# The Decameron

# 𝕾cripta 𝕳umanistica

Directed by
BRUNO M. DAMIANI
*The Catholic University of America*

## ADVISORY BOARD

# The Decameron

*Giovanni Boccaccio*

An English Adaptation by C. Gariano

𝔖cripta 𝔥umanistica

The Classic for the Modern Reader

28

© 1986 by Carmelo Gariano

    (Scripta humanistica; 28)
    I. Boccaccio, Giovanni, 1313-1375. Decamerone.
II. Title. III. Series.
PS3557.A7155D4    1986    813'.54    86-61548
ISBN 0-916379-37-X


    *Publisher and Distributor:*
    **SCRIPTA HUMANISTICA**
    1383 Kersey Lane
    Potomac, Maryland 20854 U.S.A.



    © Giovanni Boccaccio
Library of Congress Catalog Card Number 86-61548
International Standard Book Number 0-916379-37-X

*To Dr. Bob H. Suzuki,*

*for his efforts to raise academic excellence at CSUN by supporting the faculty members committed to teaching, research and publishing*

*C. Gariano*

# Acknowledgements

This work has been published thanks to a subvention from the California State University, Northridge. My special thanks go to a few people associated with this institution of higher learning, namely: Dr. Patrick Kennicott, director of Research and Sponsored Projects; Dr. Steve Oppenheimer, chairman of the School Research Committee, and the other members of this committee who supported my request. I am also thankful to Mrs. Patricia Boles for securing supplementary funds within the School of Humanities and, above all, to the dean of the School, Dr. Jerome Richfield, without whose help I would have found it hard to publish my last three books, including this one. I want to express my sincere gratitude to Ms. Sandra Christenson, an English instructor at CSUN, for editing the manuscript, as well as to Cynthia Carpenter, Barbara Mathews, and Rama Kalminov for their valuable assistance.

BY THE SAME AUTHOR (C. GARIANO):

**Criticism:**
1. *Análisis estilístico de los "Milagros de Nuestra Señora" de Berceo.* 2nd. ed. Madrid: Gredos, 1973.
2. *El mundo poético de Juan Ruiz.* 2nd. ed. Madrid: Gredos, 1975.
3. *El enfoque estilístico y cultural de las obras medievales.* Madrid: Ediciones Alcalá, 1968.
4. *La lírica italiana en el siglo XX.* Buenos Aires: La Porteña, 1967.
5. *Juan Ruiz, Boccaccio, Chaucer.* Sacramento: The Hispanic Press, 1985.
6. *La Edad Media. Aproximación alfonsina.* Washington: Scripta Humanistica, 1986.

**Texts:**
7. *Spanish for You. The Teacher's Guide.* 2 vols. Hollywood, 1967. (Text with thirty films for an elementary Spanish course, produced by Lingua/Film, Inc.)

**Editions:**
8. *Sagrada Biblia.* Edition "Hogar Católico." Mexico, Chicago: The Catholic Press, Inc., 1958.
9. *Diccionario de Información bíblica.* Mexico, Chicago: The Catholic Press, Inc., 1958.

**Poetry:**
10. *Añicos del laúd iridiscente.* Madrid: Gredos, 1968.
11. *Saga de Kennedy.* (Elegies) Los Angeles: Orbe, 1966.
12. *Anhelos, búsquedas y encuentros.* Madrid: Gredos, 1966.

**Copyrighted Theater:**
13. *The Last Troubadour.* (Provençal music by T. Miller)
14. *Incesto y redención.*
15. *The Cunning Sheik.* (Commedia dell'arte.)

**Ready for the Press:**
16. *An Eye for an Aye.* (Novel)

# Foreword

It is customary to inform the reader that Giovanni Boccaccio was born in 1313 in Paris of a French mother and a Florentine merchant father. His growth zigzagged along with the unstable route of Florence's mercantile empire in the fourteenth century and brought him from such whereabouts as the arms of whimsical Maria D'Aquino, the illegitimate daughter of King Robert of Naples, to the mischievous rejection of a pleasant widow.

Intriguing as it may be, Boccaccio's life is but a chain of episodes, a savings account whose interest is shared in his literary production. What really counts is his artistic significance. He stands for a masterpiece that has had a decisive impact on the renewal of taste in Europe. Compared to Dante, Cervantes or Shakespeare, he is not a genius reaching the same level of universality, but he has universal appeal and has been a steady presence through the last six centuries of fictional literature.

Opposed to Dante's masterpiece, his *Decameron* has been considered the human comedy, the *Arabian Nights* of Italian literature developing a different mode of the Mediterranean sensitivity, the earthly bible contrasting the spiritual message of the Holy Writ. This great book is not a simple collection of one hundred short stories framed within the unifying context of the black plague. It is a new vision of life through art. People of the past had identified happiness with supernatural salvation; Boccaccio identifies it with the worldly destiny of man. Life is no longer a unidirectional ascent from earth to heaven. It unfolds as a complex network of relations and runs a wide

1

gamut of antinomies and contradictions.

In the *Decameron*, Boccaccio captures objectivity using the storyteller's detachment and molds it into a congenial form of art. His vision of life becomes as wide as life itself and turns into a concrete form of poetry by leaning on authentic experiences that encompass variety within unity. Aristocrats and rogues, scholars and prostitutes, clergymen and rascals are displayed in his extensive gallery of characters.

Actually, none of these characters rises to epic levels, although most of them have tridimensional proportions, vivid movements, and intense feelings. They all show Boccaccio's interest in everyday man engaged in a constant challenge to the rigid structures of an unquestioned culture. His orientation stresses change and renewal—change from the static center of ancient life, renewal into a pluricentric conception of life. Thus man integrates himself in a convergence of paradox and rationality. Virtue is still a lifting force, but vice is not narrowly condemned. It becomes another ingredient of art, enticing man towards a new morality in which the loss of innocence is rewarded by the gain of insight and maturity.

The *Decameron* erupted into life with the same urge as the life which floods the artistic structure of the work. Its content is vital. And so is its message. Its kinship is with the spiritually young, for they feel and act spontaneously. The author cannot repress his distaste for moral ankylosis that stiffens growth in those who are twisted and who try to twist others. For instance, in the twentieth tale, what makes old Master Richard ridiculous is not his decision to marry a young and sexy wife in his old age, but his stuffy arguments repressing her legitimate craving for pleasure. In the forty-fourth tale, what makes the whole situation laughable is not the tender girl who hands her virginity to her first lover by duping her parents, but her old folks who cannot face reality with a straightforward gaze, preferring to hide behind the shield of insincerity.

In this masterpiece, life becomes a constant craving for happiness. Like life, love unfolds by living, by exciting the springs of action. Since the soul expresses itself thanks to the body, the harmony of physical features is much more than an aesthetic image. It is a reflection of inner life. Through passion, love conditions life to the same extent that life conditions love. Their interplay becomes the main force that refines man. For the roots of civilization seem to be planted in the human heart. Simply put, as man strives to better himself in order to deserve the heart of a beautiful woman, he expands his creativity and makes this a better world. That's the lesson imparted by the forty-first tale in the *Decameron*, when Cimon advances from primitivism to refinement after he admires a sleeping beauty and feels suddenly invaded by the internal agent that unchains the full range of human energies and widens the sphere of human values.

Under the sign of Boccaccesque art, passion has often been misjudged as a refined kind of erotic delight, although it goes far beyond its erotic content. Actually, it is a drive that frees men from useless taboos, reconciling them both to the war of the sexes and the peace of sex. Tenderness compensates strength. Tolerance smooths jealousy. Comprehension thwarts revenge. Satisfied passion makes love more meaningful, consequently modifying life and man's view of it.

That explains why Boccaccio's outlook is basically optimistic. Smiles and laughter are specific human manifestations associated with such a philosophy of life. And we are made to laugh and smile as the author coats irony with understanding breadth, drowns hate out of his work, and sketches human beings by portraying the corruption of the clergy, the presumption of foolish husbands, the tricks of impassioned women, the absurdity of superstitions, and the duplicity of both impotent and powerful people.

The *Decameron*, a sequence of one hundred stories within a contrived frame, has an artistic unity of its own. It re-establishes art's autonomy from religion and morals, thus opening the roads of humanism. It enlarges the world of culture and injects a glimmer of paganism into the Christian outlook of life, thus foreshadowing a peek into the present-day dilemma. By pointing to life, art contributes to its enrichment. Its narrative is meant to beautify even the sinful acts of daily life by inducing the practice of virtue without evoking ethical constraint. Thus it is the beginning of men's and women's liberation by stressing free choice in love. Boccaccio is definitely modern, one of the very first modern men in the Middle Ages, although his message is still clothed in the stylistic categories of the past. He openly confesses that he wrote to bring relief and release to the sad condition of medieval women who could escape their isolation from the mainstream of activity and thought mainly by reading.

Reading, in the past, was a way of gathering copious details interspersed in the slow progress of the action. Reading aloud and leisurely was a way of enlivening the blend of detailed descriptions, relaxed transitions, verbose sermons, lengthy series of rhetorical questions, elaborate monologues and long dialogues, although such a stylistic redundancy had its vulnerabilities.

Boccaccio himself, in the conclusion of the *Decameron*, admitted that excessive length would be mentioned as one of the flaws of his work, and justified it with an argument that was quite valid in his time. Those who had more pressing matters at hand would not read his tales no matter how short they might be. He also reminded his critics that he had dedicated them to ladies with plenty of time available, and none of them went in those days "to Athens, Bologna or Paris to study." Luckily times have changed, and the diffusion of knowledge has made the artistic core of his masterpiece relevant both to women and men.

The English-speaking reader of the past enjoyed reading the *Decameron* aloud as a remedy against melancholy. Today's reader is pressed for time and therefore prefers more focused materials. He/she captures reality with greater speed, though not necessarily with deeper insight. In such a context, a stylistic selectivity may give a broader comprehension of other ages by making masterpieces such as this one more relevant and accessible to modern taste. It may even make the difference between feeling forced to read an old classic and being inspired to read a rejuvenated one.

Our approach to Boccaccio's stylistic virtuosity was not simply guided by a dietary attack against literary bulge. Rather, it was inspired by a need and a wish: a need to synthesize the static past with the fleeting present and a wish to offer the compact essence of a book that represents an outstanding stage of development in Western culture.

From Chaucer's tales to *Playboy*'s cinematic evocation, Boccaccio's work has proved its literary resilience, thus justifying our attempt to apply a well-intentioned plastic surgery on its venerable stylistic wrinkles. It may destroy the original look—that is a true danger indeed. But like all cases of plastic surgery, the new appearance may help us appreciate the beauty of the old essence.

C. G.

# Table of Contents

6

# THE FIRST DAY

## Free Topics

# The Bubonic Plague

Gracious ladies, in spite of my concern for your natural short-comings, I feel obliged to remind you of a sad tragedy that struck mankind a few years ago. That was the year of the black pestilence, 1348 A.D. It was sent upon us by the just wrath of God after it spread out from the East into several places in the West. At first, it appeared as a huge swelling of the groins or armpits and, later on, it extended into other parts of the body. No medical skills were capable of preventing or healing its deadly effects. It spread like fire upon dry or greased materials and contaminated not only human beings, but also animals. I saw with my own eyes two hogs come upon some infected rags and tear them with their jaws. Soon after, both animals fell dead as if they had been poisoned.

Those people who were not contaminated came to the inhuman conclusion that they could save their lives by isolating themselves from the sick and their infected belongings. They started to live moderately and locked themselves in houses where there had been no case of infection. Others chose a different course of action and lived immoderately going day and night from one tavern to another.

Amidst the general faltering of organized life, even the ties of blood and kinship decayed. Parents refused to attend to their children, and vice versa. Servants abandoned their masters, lured by higher wages. Well-bred women lost their shame. Those who recovered from the plague underwent a total change in their moral standards.

16

People died by flocks without receiving the benefit of the sacraments or the usual services of a religious burial. As the pestilence grew in rigor, human bodies were heaped in the churchyards by layers and covered with some soil. At the same time, the peasants abandoned their crops and cattle in despair, and the confusion of unattended animals made more macabre the scene of death and desolation in the open fields. The pestilence decimated the population of Florence and destroyed many famous families and their great fortunes and power.

In this sad state of affairs, seven young ladies between eighteen and twenty-eight years of age gathered one Tuesday morning in the church of Santa Maria Novella in Florence. They were lovely, pleasant, and noble. For the sake of discretion, I shall omit their real names and use nicknames that reflect some of their qualities; that is, Pampinea, Fiammetta, Filomena, Emilia, Lauretta, Neifile, and Elisa.

After they said their prayers, Pampinea proposed that they take a hard look at the situation in town and decide to run away from the body count and the sad lamentation of those who survived. Considering that even nuns and monks had broken the ecclesiastical discipline to satisfy their carnal appetites before death, she suggested that they leave the city and spend their time in the country trying to obtain as much enjoyment as possible.

The other ladies accepted her advice. Filomena, without rejecting it, stressed the frail nature of women and mentioned that they needed the guidance and company of some men. It was not an easy thing to do, for men were extremely scarce. While they were musing over their plan, three young men, all of them over twenty-five years old, entered the church. They were Panfilo, Filostrato, and Dioneo, three loving gentlemen whose sweethearts were among the seven girls planning to leave town. As soon as the ladies saw them, they felt more hopeful about carrying out their decision and expressed it to them. The gentlemen accepted gladly.

On the following Wednesday, they went to a villa located on a low hill about two miles away from Florence. It was a neatly kept place with a wide supply of food and beverages. Dioneo, who was a happy-go-lucky young man, proposed to ban all worrying from their lives. Pampinea accepted his advice and suggested that they elect

17

one of them to rule over the others and work out a program of diversions for the first day. He or she would then appoint a successor to arrange the program for the next day.

She was made queen of the group and a laurel garland was placed on her head as a visible sign of her royal authority. First things first, she distributed the chores among the servants. Then the group went sporting and organized some other kind of fun. At last, Pampinea ruled that they should entertain one another by telling stories in accordance with a subject previously assigned. The idea was unanimously approved, and only Dioneo was excused from the obligation to stick to the subject matter. Due to his humorous skill, he was supposed to deliver the last story of each day, thus providing a happy finale to the group narration. For ten days during the two weeks spent in the villa, they repeated a total of one hundred stories in daily sequence, except Friday in memory of the Lord and Saturday in reverence to His Blessed Mother.

The narrative plan unfolded as follows: (a) The first day, with Pampinea as queen, was taken with free topics; (b) The second day, under Filomena's rule, concerned the cases of people affected by different shifts of fortune who came at last to a happy ending beyond their expectations; (c) The third day, under Neifile, dealt with the turns of events in which people by dint of diligence satisfied their wishes or recovered some lost goods; (d) The fourth day, under Filostrato, touched upon tragic love stories; (e) The fifth day, under Fiammetta, had to do with the happy ending occurring to lovers after cruel and woeful adventures; (f) The sixth day, with Elisa as queen, dealt with the witty answers of people who had been attacked with gibing speeches; (g) The next day, under Dioneo, was dedicated to the tricks that women play on their own husbands for love or self-preservation; (h) The eighth day, under Lauretta, dealt with the tricks that women play all day long against men and vice versa; (i) The ninth day, under Emilia, called for free topics; and (j) The tenth day, under Panfilo, dealt with the deeds of those who have behaved magnificently in matters of love and other noble endeavors. Let's now follow the unfolding plan of their narrative.

# 1.  The Fake Sanctified

Sir Franzesi was a respected businessman who had lived for many years in France. Due to his personal merits, he was knighted by the king of France and late in his life decided to retire to Italy. Consequently, he untangled himself from his commercial commitments and transferred his functions to an able manager. He still had some loans to recover from the Burgundians, but he could not find the right man for such a transaction. He knew that the Burgundians were quarrelsome and disloyal, and wondered whom he could send to take care of his interests among those people.

Suddenly he recalled a man who was the right match for their wickedness. It was Master Ciappelleto, an Italian escrow agent, who was called Sir Chapelet by the French people. He was a nasty little fellow, usually neatly dressed, who had had troubles both with private parties and with the law because of his malice. He derived special delight from writing faulty deeds in property sales, bearing false witness, assaulting innocent people, and cursing God and his sacraments. He did not care for women, but indulged in the opposite perversion. A glutton and a drinker, he also was a notorious gambler with cogged dice. No wonder he immediately accepted Sir Franzesi's proposal to deal with those wicked people from Burgundy.

Contrary to his violent temper, he began to soft-pedal his approach as a collector, reserving his angry outburts as a last resort. He lived in Burgundy with two Florentine brothers, both moneylenders, who entertained him with great honor because of Sir Franzesi. Before long, Master Chapelet happened to fall ill, and the two brothers secured the best medical care for him. Yet he grew worse and worse because of his past abuses and disorderly life.

The two moneylenders started to worry, for they were confronted with a serious dilemma. After so much attention, how could they throw him out of their house without causing a scandal? On the

19

other hand, they were whispering, "This wicked man will never take the sacraments of the church. Therefore, at his death, he'll be dumped into a ditch like a dog. And if he confesses, again he'll be dumped into a ditch, because no confessor will grant him absolution. In either case," they concluded, "the local population will hate us more. They will have a good excuse to pillage our business and endanger our lives."

"Never mind," reacted Master Chapelet, who overheard their concerned conversation. He had become quick of hearing as often happens to the sick. Then he continued, "Go and bring me the holiest confessor, and I'll take care of the rest." Although hopeless, they brought him a most worthy monk, who sat alone beside the moribund and started to take the confession.

"How long since you last confessed?"

"Father, I used to confess at least once a week or more. Lately my sickness has prevented me from doing so for eight days."

"Well done, son, well done. It won't take long for you to confess your sins."

"Oh, no, Father. I want to make a general confession of all my sins as far back as I can remember. Ask me all the questions you want. Never mind my sickness. I'd rather displease my flesh than lose my soul." Pleased, the holy man asked if he had ever sinned for lust with a woman. The roguish sinner replied: "Father, I am afraid to sin of vainglory by saying the truth. But I'll tell you. I am still as virgin as I came out of my mother's womb."

"Blessed be of God! You deserve more credit than we clergy because you have done so without being forced by vows or rules. Now tell me. Have you sinned by way of gluttony?"

"Yes, I have, and quite often. I used to fast on Lent and other times, too. Yet, whenever I drank water after working, I relished it as drinkers do alcohol. And when I had my meals, I enjoyed them in a way that no devout faster should."

"That's natural," commented the confessor.

"Natural?" rejoined Master Chapelet. "Don't give me that line! You know that things done for God must be done willingly. Otherwise, it is sinful." The holy man was pleased. Then he asked if the had ever sinned of usury.

"Father, don't take me for one of these usurers. I have nothing to do with them. I was born in a rich home. Whatever profit I made in my business, I always shared with the poor."

"Have you ever sinned of anger?"

"Oh," cried Chapelet. "Who can refrain from anger when you see so many people haunting the taverns instead of going to church?"

"Son, that is a righteous wrath. Now tell me, did you ever commit manslaughter?"

"How can you say that? You, a man of God. Do you think the Lord would let me prosper?"

"Have you spoken ill of anyone?"

"Oh yes, Father. I had a bad neighbor. He used to beat his poor wife. Once I felt sorry for her and went to speak against him before her relatives."

"You did the right thing," said the monk. "By the way, you said that you are a merchant. Did you ever cheat your customers?"

"Once I did. A customer paid for his purchase. He left four pennies more than he should. When I realized his mistake, he was already gone and never came back. I kept the coins for one year. Finally, I gave them away in alms."

The monk was ready to give the absolution, but the wicked man detained him. He had more sins in stock. Once he had his servant sweep the house on a Sunday, the very day of the Lord. Another time, unthinkingly, he spat on the church.

"That's nothing," smiled the confessor. "We clergy spit there all day long."

"That's too bad," replied Master Chapelet. "Nobody should do so in the church of God." And after a deep sigh, he broke into a burst of weeping. He had a big sin to confess, a sin he had always been ashamed to admit because he felt God would not forgive him. The confessor kept insisting. Master Chapelet continued to weep. Finally, he confessed. When he was a kid, he had cursed his mother.

"Son, don't cry. Such is your contrition that the Lord will forgive you."

"How can you be so sure? Cursing my mother, my sweet mother. Please, pray for me." There he ended, and the religious man absolved him, convinced that he was a holy son of God. In the meantime, the two brothers listened in disbelief to this confession from a paneling that divided the chamber. They hardly refrained from laughing, pleased as they were with the result.

21

Master Chapelet died a few days later, and the two brothers paid for a religious burial. The confessor informed the prior and his brethren of what he had gathered from that confession. He persuaded his credulous colleagues to receive Chapelet's body with reverence in the hope that God should show many miracles through him. It so happened that the gullible monk inflamed the populace with devotion. They all believed his sanctity and flocked to kiss his feet. Then, they started to bring candles and images. In a short time, Master Chapelet became Saint Chapelet and worked miracles aplenty for those who solemnly vowed unto him.

## 2. The Converted Jew

John de Chevigny was a Parisian dealing in silks and stuffs. He was a close friend to a rich Jew, Abraham, a merchant and a very honest man. Like all Catholics, John de Chevigny was irked at the idea that such a good Jew should lose his soul for lack of faith, so he started to entreat him to turn Catholic and missed no chance to pressure him. Merchants are very direct in their ways, yet Abraham resisted all his attempts. At last the Jew, overcome by such insistence, promised that he would go to Rome and consider the manners of God's Vicar upon earth and his chief brethren.

John was chagrined at his words. He knew that even a Catholic might abandon his beliefs if he saw the lewd life of the Roman clergy. But there was no way to sway Abraham's determination to go to see the Holy See.

Once in Rome, Abraham began to inquire into the life of the pope, cardinals, and other prelates of the Roman court. Being a quick-witted man, he found out that all of them, from the lowest to the highest, were shamefully given to lust, not only according to nature, but also in a homosexual fashion. The influence of high prostitutes and pederasts was essential in attaining any kind of favor. The Roman clergy were gluttons, drinkers, and greedy. For money, they would sell human blood, yes, even Christian blood, and all ecclesiastical benefices. They employed, for such business, more brokers in Rome than there were commercial agents in Paris. They called "procuration" their traffic and "sustentation" their gluttony, as if God might de duped by their semantic gimmicks.

The Jewish merchant, a decent and sober man, was fed up. When John saw him on his return, he had no hope that Abraham would become a Christian. But the latter had a surprise in store for him. Judging from the leaders of Christianity, everyone seemed to be engaged in destroying the very faith they were supposed to support. Yet, it continually increased and grew more glorious. "I manifestly discern," concluded Abraham, "that the Holy Spirit is the true support of the Catholic Church. Therefore, it must be the true and holy religion above all, and I am ready to embrace it."

John de Chevigny, looking for a different outcome, was overjoyed at such an unexpected turn. It goes without saying that he was Abraham's sponsor during his baptism at Notre Dame Church in Paris.

## 3. The Jewish Moneylender

Saladin, famous for his power and victories among Saracens and Christians, was in dire need of a large sum of money. He knew that Melchisedek, a Jewish moneylender, had the means to help him. But he also knew that Melchisedek was tight with his money and would not oblige him of his own free will. He decided to force him by coloring his motives with some show of reason. Accordingly, when the rich and learned Jew was in his presence, he set his trap and asked which of the three religions he considered the true one: the Jewish, the Christian, or the Moslem. The moneylender sensed that the sultan was entrapping him in words as a pretext to blackmail him, so he sharpened his wits and speedily came out with an appropriate tale to avoid the danger.

"My lord, to answer your question, let me tell you a little story. A very rich man had a precious ring. His three sons were good and virtuous. They knew the value of the ring, and each one wanted it for himself. The old man loved them all alike and was not able to make up his mind and choose one among the three. Before dying, he secretly called a craftsman and had him make two more rings so like the original that it was impossible to discern which was which. Then he secretly gave each son his ring. After the father's death, each one believed he was the true heir, but which one received the true ring is an open question. Likewise the three religions were given by God, and all people deem themselves to be the heirs of the true faith."

Saladin perceived how subtle the Jewish moneylender had been in avoiding the snare laid at his feet. Therefore, he openly confessed his intention. Melchisedek helped him freely with his money and gained his royal favors.

# 4.   The Lewd Abbot

Long ago, there lived a young friar in a Lunigian monastery whose lustiness could be tamed neither by fasting nor by vigils. On a sunny day, while the others slept, he went out alone. Suddenly he spotted a well-favored lady and felt the imperious pricks of carnal appetite. He accosted her and started a casual chat that, from one topic to another, led to a common agreement.

While they were consorting in the friar's cell, their merriment attracted the attention of the abbot who happened to pass by. The old man recognized a lady's voice and felt like opening the door, but suspected that she might be the wife or daughter of some powerful man and took a more discreet course of action. He went back to his cell to await the young friar. This one, although absorbed by the pleasurable company, heard a scuffling of feet before his door and, through a crevice, realized that the abbot was hearkening, surely aware of the woman's presence. But he did not show his chagrin. At last, he told the girl to wait until he came back, for he would find a way to let her out unperceived.

He went out, locked the door, and headed straight towards the abbot's cell. There he handed him the key, adding that he was going to have some work done. The abbot took the key and gave him leave to go. Then he went to the friar's cell.

The girl, aghast, burst into tears. But she was young and pretty, and the abbot succumbed to her charm. He kissed and embraced her. Then, he mounted the friar's bed. Having regard for both the grave burden of his dignity and the lady's tender age, he did not lie on her. He preferred to set her upon himself and have fun for a long while.

The young friar viewed his superior's performance with an eager sense of relief. At the end, the abbot locked the girl in the cell and went back to his chamber. When the young friar came for his key, the abbot started to rebuke him, threatening to cast him into prison, so he might enjoy the prey alone.

"Sir," answered the young friar with calm. "I haven't been long enough in the Benedictine Order to learn all the rules of penance and discipline. Now you have shown me that we should let our bodies be crushed by women as we do with fasts and vigils. I will always follow your good example."

Caught in his own snare, the abbot let the girl out with great secrecy. From then on, no one ever cared how often she was allowed into the monastery as long as it was done with discretion.

## 5. The Marchioness's Reproof

The marquis of Monferrato was a noble man and a worthy warrior. He had just gone overseas on the occasion of a general crusade undertaken by the Christians against the Moors. Once he was praised at the court of the French king, Philip the Borgne (The One-eyed). Most courtiers extolled his wife's virtue, the marchioness of Monferrato, the fairest and noblest of all the ladies in the world. Moved by these words, King Philip decided to depart for the same crusade from the port of Genoa. Thus he could journey by land and have a chance to visit with the marchioness.

When he came close to her palace, he dispatched a courier to announce his royal visit. She openly welcomed this great favor, but wondered what such a visit could mean in her husband's absence. It was not long before she ascertained the king's real motives. Nevertheless, she received him with great honor.

At dinner time, the dignitaries occupied different tables. The king sat at one table with the lady, exceedingly admiring her charm and manners. At a certain point he realized that, although there was a variety of dishes, they were all hens cooked and seasoned in different fashions. He turned to the beautiful lady with a merry air and asked her, "Madame, are only hens born in these parts without ever a rooster?" The marchioness was happy to be asked the expected question and promptly answered the passionate king: "No, my lord. But women, although in dress and dignity they may differ somehow from others, are the same here as elsewhere."

The king understood the answer very well and found out the true meaning of that uniform meal. He knew that it would be of no avail to waste words on her. Violence was out of the question. So he finished discreetly and, by his quick departure, made amends for that unwise visit.

## 6.  A Greedy Inquisitor

Not too long ago, there was in our city of Florence a Minorite friar who was an inquisitor of heretical depravity. He studied to appear pious, but what he actually sought most were rich Christians with some flaws in matters of faith.

It so happened that one day a good simple man, richer in gold than wit, praised his wine to excess and dared to say that it was so good that even Christ would drink of it.

"Even Christ?" inquired the zealous inquisitor, informed of such words. His holy wrath became proportionate to the man's purse, and he was ready to nail him to a grievous suit, eager not to straighten the defendant's unorthodox views, but to milk as many florins as possible out of his pocket.

The good man admitted what he had said. The inquisitor, a devotee of St. George Goldenbeard, retorted: "So you have made Christ a drinker and wine lover as if he were a vulgar tavern haunter. That is no light matter indeed!" He stretched his threats so close to a burning pyre that the poor man was terrified. Thanks to St. George Goldenmouth's ointment—a sovereign remedy of Minorite friars— the threat of fire was commuted to a lighter penance.

Besides, the good simpleton was ordered to hear daily mass and then report to the inquisitor. One day, on hearing mass, his attention was caught by the Biblical words, "For every one ye shall receive a hundred and shall possess eternal life." Then he went to see the inquisitor, who was at the dinner table with some guests.

"Have you heard mass?" asked the rigid man of God.

"Yes, sir. I have."

"Any doubts in your mind?" continued the friar.

"Oh, no doubt at all. I do firmly believe what I heard. That's why I pity you and your brethren."

"What about?"

"You remember the Gospel, 'For every one ye shall receive a hundred?'"

"That's true."

"I feel sorry for you. Since I have been coming here, every day your friars give the poor two huge caldrons of broth instead of throwing it away. If you get back a hundred times that much, you will all be drowned in it."

Those who were at the inquisitor's table burst into laughter at this innocent statement. The inquisitor was simply incensed—now he had no grounds to saddle the simpleton with another legal suit.

# 7. Shameful Avarice

Sir Cane della Scala was a magnificent nobleman. He invited many gentlemen from all parts of Italy to a party in Verona. Then, suddenly, he changed his mind and dismissed all his guests with provisions and gifts, except one—Bergamin—who was an accomplished knight. He waited in a public lodging at his own expense. Sir Cane conceived an illogical dislike for him and gave him neither largess nor dismissal. One day he asked the unhappy knight why he was so depressed.

Bergamin had a ready answer. "My Lord, you ought to know that Primasse, a French scholar, was very famous for his knowledge and wisdom. One day he heard about the abbot of Cluny, the richest prelate after the pope. He walked over twelve miles to see the magnificence of this abbot, and took three cakes of bread in case he arrived after dinner. Luckily, he arrived on time and sat at the table with the other guests. The first person the abbot saw on entering the dining room was Primasse, who was not well dressed. 'Look upon whom I waste my food,' thought the prelate, and turned away hoping that the unknown guest would tire of waiting and leave. Primasse was determined to see the abbot. Since no food was served until the prelate sat at the table, the scholar, who was hungry, started to eat his bread cakes one by one. This perseverance was reported to the abbot who felt guilty for his sudden avarice. He had freely given hospitality to so many people, small and great, noble and scoundrel, and now was annoyed by a man of little account. Wishing to know who he was, the abbot went to face the unknown guest and found out he was Primasse. Surprised, he made amends and treated him well, with money, clothes, and a horse."

Sir Cane understood the message and acted accordingly.

31

## 8. The Scorned Merchant

Master Hermin Grimaldi was believed to be the wealthiest merchant in Italy, but he was also the most miserly being on earth. In fact, he was nicknamed Hermin Avarice.

One day a well-known minstrel, William Borsiere, came to Genoa. In those times, minstrels were well-bred people. They negotiated treaties, transacted marriages, combined alliances, and solaced the courts with pleasant sayings. Our minstrel was honored by all the gentlemen of Genoa. Master Hermin, in spite of his avarice, wished to see him, too. He received the minstrel with friendly words and, conversing of various topics, led him and the rest of the company to his new house, a beautiful home indeed. After showing the house, he ventured a question: "Master William, you have traveled and seen a great deal. Can you tell me something unheard of or unseen that I may have some artist paint in one of these rooms?"

"Something unheard of? Unseen?" pondered the minstrel.

"Yes, something I have never heard of, nor seen," replied Master Hermin.

"Liberality!" exclaimed William the minstrel.

## 9. A Rebuked King

A gentlewoman of Gascony, on her way back from a trip to the Holy Places, stopped at Cyprus. There she was abused by some lewd fellows and received no satisfaction from the public authorities. No use complaining to the king of the island, for he was a coward, tolerant of any kind of affront. Despairing of redress, she appeared in tears before the king.

"My lord," she said, "I expect no satisfaction for the wrongs I received. I know you endure yours with patience. Please teach me how I can stand mine which, gladly, I would like to unload on such a patient bearer."

The inept king awoke as if from sleep and avenged the woman, henceforth prosecuting all crimes in his territory with justice and rigor.

# 10.  A Wise Man in Love

A few years ago there lived in Bologna a great physician whose name was Master Albert. Although he was almost seventy, such was the vivacity of his spirit that he felt inflamed with love upon seeing a beautiful lady called Marguerite Ghisolieri. And such was the prick of his passion that he started to act like a young lad, passing continually before her house either on foot or by horse. She got wind of his feelings and would often have a laugh alone or with other ladies.

One day, she and her girl friends decided to ridicule him because of his passion. Accordingly, they received him in a shady courtyard and treated him well. Then, they asked him how he had come to fall in love with such a fair lady. Courteously attacked, he justified his noble passion.

"Old people have more knowledge and experience than young folks. I'll tell you why I fell in love with a beautiful lady courted by many gallants. I have seen you ladies eat leeks. Now, except for its head, the leek has a bad taste. Yet, you ladies usually hold the head in your hands and munch the harsh leaves. How can one know about your taste in choosing a lover?"

The lady admired the physician's answer and accepted his decent attentions.

# THE SECOND DAY

Mishaps with a Happy Ending

# 11.  Assumed Miracle

Arrigo was a poor German attendant from Treviso. At the very moment he was expiring his soul, the bells of the cathedral started to ring by themselves. Believing this to be an omen, the people of the town proclaimed Arrigo a saint and brought his body to the church. A large crowd of blind and invalid people flocked there, hoping to be cured by touching the body.

At the same time, three Florentine clowns arrived in the excited town. They were clowns who traveled from court to court in order to amuse princes and dignitaries by doing funny impersonations and mimicking people with strange grimaces and gestures. Marveling at the huge crowd, they left their luggage at the inn and came back to satisfy their curiosity. The place was so packed with people and policemen that there was no way to reach the church and peek at the body of the holy man. One of the three Florentines, named Martellin, had a sudden idea and told his two companions, "I'll pretend to be a cripple, and you will carry me up to the saint so he may heal me."

The suggestion was accepted. They withdrew to a secluded place where Martellin grotesquely twisted his hands, fingers, legs, eyes, and mouth in a frightening way. His companions, showing utmost anxiety, took up the palsied fellow and set off for the church, asking people to make room for them. Everyone was most cooperative.

After a while, among the general expectation, Martellin started slowly to open one finger, then a hand; after that he stretched an arm and, little by little, all of his muscles returned to normal.

By chance, among those credulous believers there was a Florentine merchant who recognized Martellin as soon as he became

36

normal again. Amused, he started to laugh at the clown and exclaimed: "Confound him! Who wouldn't believe he was in truth palsied?"

"Wasn't he?" asked a Trevisian bystander.

"God forbid! He is as healthy as you are. But he is a skilled contortionist and knows how to play all kinds of tricks."

A group of people who overheard this conversation felt duped and exploded in anger. Suddenly they pushed toward Martellin, grabbed him by the hair, and kicked him. The rest of the crowd followed their example. Even his two friends, fearing for themselves, started to yell with the crowd to kill him. At the same time, they devised a way to save him from the mob.

One of them went to a police officer and accused Martellin. "That scoundrel has stolen my purse with a hundred florins." Immediately, a dozen policemen broke through the murderous mob and dragged Martellin, bruised as he was, to the police station. Many people followed and, on hearing that he was a pickpocket, started to accuse him of other robberies.

The judge was a sour man. He cross-examined Martellin, but the latter took the whole matter jestingly. Incensed, the judge had him tied up and lashed, after which he expected a confession so he might send Martellin to the gallows. Again the judge asked if the charges were true. Martellin realized that it was useless to deny them. "My lord," he answered, "I will confess everything. But first have those accusers state when and where I stole their money." The judge called them. One said that he had been robbed a week before; another, a few days ago; and someone else stated that very day.

"They lie!" exclaimed Martellin. "I have just arrived at this town for the first time. As soon as I arrived, I went to see the holy body in the church and you can see the way they treated me. You may check the register at the inn where I am lodged. If that isn't the truth, you can torture or kill me." The judge, who had a deep-seated bias against Florentines, was inflexible.

Martellin's friends, seeing him fall from the frying pan into the fire, went back to the inn and told their misfortune to the host. Laughing, he took them to an Italian merchant who was on good terms with the governor and saved the contortionist from playing his last act on the gallows.

37

## 12. What a Night!

Reynold was riding toward Verona with his servant when he ran into a company of people who appeared to be merchants. Actually, they were highway robbers. As soon as they discovered that Reynold was a merchant, they decided to rob him at the right moment and place. Therefore, they did their best to treat him kindly, thus earning his confidence.

Reynold considered himself lucky to meet them, and they all kept on riding toward a town which was a few miles away. On the way, they talked of everyday topics and, at a certain point, the subject of prayers was touched upon. One of the three highwaymen asked Reynold what kind of prayers he would say during a journey.

"Oh, I am an old-fashioned person," answered Reynold. "I just say some prayers to St. Julian and to God and all his saints to help me find a good lodging for the coming night, and they usually do. I never skip my morning prayer during a journey. Otherwise, I wouldn't feel confident of finding a good place at night."

"And did you say it this morning?"

"Of course," affirmed Reynold.

"I never did," replied the highwayman. "We'll see tonight who has better luck—you, with your prayer, or me, without one."

While fording a river, the three knaves spotted the right place for their robbery and stole everything, leaving Reynold with only a shirt on. His cowardly servant ran away, of course, and reached the town before the drawbridges were raised. Poor Reynold started to run toward the town, trying to fight the cold and hoping to reach his servant before darkness overtook him. No luck. He didn't arrive on time to be admitted. In despair, he started to look for some sort of shelter to survive the cold night. He spotted a house outside the walls of the

38

town and ran there. The door was shut. He gathered some straw at the entrance and, weeping and complaining to St. Julian, prepared to spend a sad night.

However, Reynold's patron saint had not forgotten him. The house belonged to a young and charming lady whose husband had died a short time before. She had prepared a warm bath and a good meal to spend the night with Marquis Azzo, who was in love with her and who occasionally would come to sweeten her loneliness. Suddenly, he had to break his engagement with his lovely mistress because unexpected business had forced him to go elsewhere. The frustrated lady was brooding. As soon as she stepped into her bath, she heard crying come from the front door and sent her maid to find out what it was. When she came back with the news, the compassionate lady told her to offer the hot bath to the poor man and help him as best she could.

Reynold found new reasons to thank St. Julian. The bath restored his spirit and charm. He was a handsome, tall man in the prime of life. He wore a suit belonging to the lady's late husband, which fitted him well. He was well-mannered, too, and the maid relayed her impression to the lady.

She invited Reynold to come close to enjoy the fire in the hearth, and both chatted graciously. She had heard about Reynold's servant and assured him he would find the man the next day. At the same time, her repressed desires for the marquis were still vaguely active in her blood, and the unexpected presence of this engaging man enlivened them. She often cast her eyes on him and found his person to her liking. After a delightful supper, she went to deliberate with her maid, who didn't fail to encourage her toward her drift. When she came back, she addressed Reynold, who was absorbed by a spell of temporary melancholy.

"Cheer up," she said. "Seeing you in that attire reminds me of my late husband, and I have felt like kissing you a hundred times. I am only afraid to displease you."

Reynold caught the sparkle in her eyes and needed no more words. After countless kisses and embraces, they went to bed and many times celebrated the delight of that eventful encounter. Early in the morning he received a gift from her. Then he wore some old clothes and went to the gate of the town, feigning he was coming from far away. It wasn't hard to find his servant. Not only that, but he even ran into his robbers, who were arrested and all his belongings were returned to him.

From then on, Reynold's faith in Saint Julian suffered no more crises.

## 13. The Disguised Abbot

Three young Florentine brothers were left rich by the sudden death of their father. After the shock of such a loss, they decided to live it up. And live it up they did. But finally their treasure was almost exhausted, and poverty opened the eyes which wealth had kept closed. Under pressure, they sold whatever estate was left and moved privily to London. There they became moneylenders and, after a few years of favorable business, made a fortune and went back to Florence to resume their old mode of living.

To secure a constantly high income, they left a trustworthy nephew, Alexander, in charge of their business in London. Unfortunately, a civil war between the king of England and his son polarized the country into two opposite factions, and Alexander's business dropped. His uncles in Florence had to declare bankruptcy. They lost their credit and were jailed.

Things became worse and worse for Alexander who had to run away from England to save his life. On his way back to Italy, he saw an abbot of white friars traveling with a large household and luggage. He recognized two knights of the court and was admitted to their company. He tried to find out about the abbot, for he had never seen him in London, and was confidentially informed that he was going to Rome to get a dispensation from the pope and be confirmed with ecclesiastical dignity in spite of his young age.

During the trip the abbot became acquainted with Alexander and was pleased by his good manners and handsome person. Day by day, the abbot grew more and more fond of the young merchant and sympathized with the misfortunes he had suffered in England. One night they stopped in a small town not very well supplied with lodgings. Alexander knew an innkeeper and secured the best comfort for the abbot and his friars. When finally he asked for his own room, the host told him: "Too bad. You see that every place is

41

taken. I can only accommodate you in a corner of the abbot's room."

"How can I go there?" asked Alexander dryly. "You know the abbot wants to sleep alone."

"That's how things stand," concluded the host. "The abbot is now sleeping, and you can lie there quietly."

Actually, the abbot was not sleeping and heard the dialogue with exceeding merriment, for he had conceived an ardent desire for Alexander. He called to him, whispering, and invited him to share his bed. Alexander put up many excuses at first, but ended by accepting. As soon as he got into bed, the young abbot started to pet him amorously. Alexander was both irked and shocked, thinking that he had taken up with a sexually perverted clergyman. The other divined his suspicion and smiled. Then, he took Alexander's hand and placed it on his breast. Realizing that the assumed abbot was a woman, the merchant recovered from his surprise and seized her in his arms.

"Hold it!" she exclaimed. "I am a maid. I am going to see the pope to be granted a husband, and here I am in love with you. If you agree to marry me, I'll gladly be your wife." Alexander quickly figured out that she was a noble woman and saw that she was beautiful. He answered that he would comply with her wishes. The lady was very pleased and put a ring on his finger. Then they pledged the matrimonial vows before a painting of the Lord and began their secret honeymoon to the great pleasure of both.

A few days after their arrival in Rome, the pope received the lady with Alexander and the two noblemen of her retinue. There she told His Holiness that she had fled with a great treasure from her father, the king of England, who wanted to marry her to the old prince of Scotland. She was coming to Rome to receive a husband from the pope. But on her way God had given her the man she should marry—she pointed to Alexander—and she had taken him as her partner. He was a worthy man, although he did not descend from royal lineage. Alexander was amazed at such a revelation. The two knights felt duped and became incensed. The pope, too, marveled at the lady's attire and her choice, but there was no rescinding what had happened.

A few days later, Alexander was officially married to his princess. In his splendid attire, he showed no trace of the former moneylender. A shrewd man, he managed his new condition adroitly. His relatives' fortunes were reinstated. He regained the king's favor and was made earl of Cornwall. He even reconciled the king with his rebel son and gained the love and support of all the people in the country.

# 14. The Lucky Corsair

Landolph Ruffolo had plenty of money. Yet he could not resist his speculative drive to make more, and while seeking to double his capital, he exposed himself to the danger of losing everything, even his life. He bought a big ship, loaded it with merchandise, and sailed for Cyprus. There he found the market flooded with the same kind of goods and was driven to financial ruin. Trying to save as much as he could, he sold his large boat and bought a smaller vessel which he armed properly for piracy against Turkish ships. Fortune was kinder to him in plundering than in trading. Thus he got back all he had lost and even doubled his previous holdings. Satisfied, he put an end to his pirating and decided to return home.

While sailing, a violent storm forced him to take refuge in a small harbor. There he was attacked by the crews of two boats who had also taken shelter from the storm. They seized him and his treasure. The next day, the ship with Landolph was wrenched by a violent wind, cast against the rocky coastline, and broken asunder. Everyone abandoned the sinking ship and grabbed floating planks. So did Landolph. He kept afloat until the next day when a chest was pushed against his plank by the waves and drove him under water. He struggled to get to the surface only to find his plank far removed. Strengthless, he reached the chest, which was near him, and kept on floating.

The next day, the strength of the wind cast him on the shore of an island where a poor woman was washing her pots and pans. There he lay unconscious. The lady put the chest on her daughter's head to take it home; then she carried the man by herself.

In a few days Landolph regained his lost energy and health. The lady told him to get his chest before he went on his own way. He had no recollection of such a chest, yet he took it, rather disappointed at its light weight. When the woman went out, he opened it and found

44

it full of precious stones. Experienced as he was by quick changes in fortune, he wrapped the stones in old rags, put them in a bag, and left the empty chest to the woman.

This time he had no problem in returning home by sea. He sold his stones and found himself twice as rich as he was at the start. Gladly he sent generous rewards to the lady who saved his life and to those who helped him on his way back.

## 15. The Duped Duper

Andrew, a merchant from Perugia, had often heard that horses were cheaper in Naples than in his own town. He took five hundred florins and went there to do business. He liked the horses at the market and did some rough bargaining. To prove that he meant business, he would display his golden florins. A beautiful Sicilian woman, a whore used to trading her body for small gains, caught sight of Andrew's purse as she went by. At the same time, an old Sicilian lady he knew ran into him and was pleased to see him.

The whore watched the meeting from a distance, then went to see the old woman and tried to extract from her anything she knew about the young horse dealer on the pretense of feminine curiosity. Later on, she dispatched her old maid and partner to find the unwary merchant. Informed that a distinguished lady of that town wished to see him, Andrew fancied himself an appealing man and anticipated a gallant adventure. The old woman led him to the house of her mistress, who came to receive him. She was beautiful and well-dressed. At first she felt carried away with passion, then kissed him tenderly and said, "Welcome to my house." Amazed, Andrew followed her inside to a perfumed room with rich curtains and furnishings. He was impressed, yet intrigued. The lady, weeping, explained that she was his sister.

"As you know," she went on, "our father lived some time in Palermo. There he met my mother, a young widow of a noble family, and they fell in love. He left my mother without marrying her when I was a small child. He never came back." Andrew remembered hearing his father speak of his long stay in Palermo and paid more attention to the lady's story.

"Once I grew up, my mother married me to a nobleman, but we had to leave Palermo because my husband belonged to the opposition party and was exiled. We moved here, to Naples, where King

46

Charles has made good the losses we suffered in Sicily." So saying, she kissed him tenderly and went on weeping. Andrew replied that he had no knowledge of this father's private life in Palermo and felt happy to discover such a noble sister. Yet, he wondered how she knew that he was in Naples.

"Simple," replied the lady. "An old woman who knew our father both in Palermo and Perugia informed me this morning. I thought it would be better to invite you to my house." Then she started to inquire about their relatives back at Perugia and mentioned them by name, thus giving a truthful ring to everything else.

Later on, Andrew said that he had an engagement with other traders, but she put on a sentimental show and went out of the room on the pretense of sending a maid to cancel the appointment. Time went by fast and Andrew had a splendid supper. She was sorry that her husband was abroad, but she knew how to honor him. Since it was rather late when Andrew rose from the table, she entreated him to spend the night at her home because Naples was no place to go around at that time of night, especially for a stranger. He was glad to remain in her company and kept on talking for a long while. Finally she left a valet at his service and withdrew with her maids to another side of the house.

As soon as Andrew found himself alone, he undressed and laid his belongings on the bed. Then he turned to the boy and asked where the washroom was.

"Over there," he pointed, and Andrew went in with absolute sureness. Alas! No sooner had he set foot on the inner floor when down he fell into a dark alley, and a full shower of ordure followed from above. There he began calling loudly for the boy. All in vain, for the valet ran to inform his mistress, who in turn hurriedly searched Andrew's clothes and rejoiced greatly upon finding the five hundred florins. Meanwhile, Andrew went around the house and started to knock at the door. At last, the old woman came to inquire who was making such a racket.

"That's me. Andrew, the brother of Madame."

"You must be drunk, good man. I know no Andrew nor what else you say. Leave in peace and let us sleep."

"What! You don't know me?" replied Andrew who was already aware of the fraud. "At least, give me back my clothes." She shut the window with a big laugh. Enraged, Andrew grabbed a stone from the street and started to knock at the door in a fit of violence. The neighbors woke up and yelled at him to let them sleep. Finally, a big bully of a man came to the window and asked with a terrifying voice, "Who is that below?"

"I am the brother of the lady of the house." replied Andrew in a fearful voice.

"Wait and see, you dirty drunkard," threatened the husky fellow, drawing back into the house. Some nearby people who knew that violent man advised Andrew to leave for his own good. In sour despair, he went away hoping to reach the inn. Having gone a few blocks, he saw two men coming forth with a lantern. Afraid that they were the police patrol, he ran into a hovel close by. They did the same, but one of them couldn't stand the smell and lifted the lantern toward Andrew, who was petrified with fear. When they found out what had happened to him, they told him to be glad he had escaped alive from that snare. Then they asked him if he would help them in a promising adventure. "This morning the late archbishop of Naples was buried in the cathedral with a ruby on his finger worth more than your five hundred florins."

Andrew followed them. As they passed by a well, they decided to lower him down and wash away his smell. Instantly some thirsty policemen came there. The two rascals ran away, and the officers began to pull the bucket from the well, wondering why it was so heavy. But when they saw a man grab the sides of the well with both hands, they dropped cord, weapons and all, running away quite frightened. Andrew, amazed and sad, didn't know which way to go.

As he walked, he met the two companions who came back for him and clarified what had happened. Then they reached the cathedral and opened the huge tomb of the archbishop, propping the heavy lid so that a man could enter.

"Now, who'll go in?" asked one of them.

"Not me," replied the other.

"Neither me," rejoined the first fellow. "Let Andrew go in."

"Oh no!" said Andrew with horror.

"You dare not?" And both looked at him with ferocious eyes and threatened him with iron bars. Andrew, tamed, crept into the tomb, suspecting that those knaves would cheat him in the end. So he took first the precious ring and put it on his finger. Then he handed them the archbishop's precious garments. "That's all,' he said after doing so.

"Look for the ring. It must be there," bid the two rogues. He kept them in suspense, feigning a careful search. Finally, they pulled the prop and left him shut in the tomb. Horrified, the poor man tried to lift up the lid. In vain! Overcome, he fell on the dead body.

At this point, he heard a group of people coming to the tomb, also to rob it. After they propped up the lid, they started to argue who should go in, but no one was ready to do so. Finally a priest said, "Why are you afraid? He won't eat you. I'll go myself." He crept to the opening and set one leg inside the tomb to jump in. Andrew grabbed the priest's leg to pull it. The other gave a terrified yell, and they all scrambled away as if pursued by a host of devils, leaving the lid raised.

Happy beyond all hope, Andrew sprang out of the tomb and reached the inn. There he found his colleagues very concerned. Soon after, he returned to his hometown satisfied that he had invested his capital in a ring, although his primary purpose was to buy horses.

## 16.  An Adventurous Mother

When Sicily was invaded by a French king, Harry Capece, a supporter of the previous monarch, was thrown into jail. His wife fled Sicily with their eight-year old son, Geoffrey, and one of her maids. They tried to reach Lipari in a small boat, but were thrown onto a solitary island by a storm. As the lady was pregnant, she bore another son, whom she named Outcast. One day she left the youngsters with the maid on the shore and went to a secluded place where she could be alone with her memories and bemoan her jailed husband. At this juncture, a pirate galley captured her children with the maid and towed away her boat.

Upon her return, the lady was taken by surprise and awe. When she realized her new disgrace, she behaved like a distressed person and fainted. Finally, she decided to survive by eating herbs and drinking water. One day she entered a cavern where she had seen a goat, and there found two newborn kidlings. In a natural impulse, she fed the two little beasts with her own breast since her milk wasn't yet dried from her recent delivery. The two young animals sucked her breast as well as the goat's, and the abandoned lady grew attached to them. She neglected herself altogether and kept on living in a natural way.

A few months later, a gentleman named Conrad of Malespini stopped on the island accompanied by his wife and some servants. He was returning from a pilgrimage to the holy place in Puglia. His dogs went after the goat, but they stopped before the cavern because the abandoned lady chased them away. Conrad saw her, and after much questioning, she repeated her sad story and confirmed her resolution to remain alone on the island. He had known Harry Capece during better times and entreated the poor woman to leave the island and go with them. She accepted and was allowed to take along the goat with the two kidlings. She went to work in the palace under an assumed name.

Her two children had been sold as slaves together with the maid, who changed the older boy's name from Geoffrey to Johnnie in order to prevent any political persecution in those changing times. A few years later, Johnnie grew up to be tall and handsome. He left his owner to improve his lot and found out that his father was still alive and was kept in jail by the new king.

Wandering at random, he came to Malespini's castle and entered his service, but never recognized his mother who was also there. The gentleman had a very charming daughter who was left a widow soon after her marriage, and the two young folks fell madly in love with each other. As their love grew, they acted bolder and bolder.

One day, the lady's father happened to come upon them while they were at the mercy of Venus in a lonely corner of the wood. He had his daughter and Johnnie arrested and would have put them to death, but the mother's intercession delayed such a sentence. The two lovers were locked in separate cells, where they stayed for over one year. Johnnie was never recognized.

At this time, the French king was kicked out of Sicily by a popular revolution supported by the king of Aragon. Malespini was happy at this turn of events because he was also against the French king. When the rumor of that political change reached Johnnie in prison, he sighed and said, "What luck! I have been living like a beggar for fourteen years, and now that my chance has come, here I am, locked in prison."

"What do you have to do in Sicily with the great kings?" inquired the jailer.

Johnnie, in despair, disclosed his identity. The honest guard reported everything he had heard to his lord, who inquired into the whole matter in detail. When he found out the truth from Johnnie (actually Geoffrey) and his mother, he announced to the young man that he would reinstate him to his previous honrable condition. However, he didn't miss the chance to reprove Geoffrey for what he had done to his daughter's honor and stressed the large dowry she had as a widow. A formal marriage would be welcome.

"Sir," replied Geoffrey with dignity, "neither lust nor greed brought me close to your daughter. I loved and always will love her dearly. If you think I wronged her, it was a consequence of young

51

age. Older people shouldn't forget their own youth. I committed it as a friend, not as an enemy."

The marriage between the two lovers was immediately sanctioned by the father. Their joy was doubled when the boy's mother was notified of the new turn of events. As it often happens, one happy step leads to another. Conrad sent two emissaries: one to rescue the younger brother from slavery, the other to contact their father in Sicily. Both missions were successful, and the family reunion was a joyful event.

## 17. The Re-virgined Princess

Alatiel was her name: the most beautiful woman in her generation. She was the daughter of the soldan of Babylon, a powerful sovereign, who was leading his country with remarkable success. Alatiel was promised as a wife to the king of Garbo who had helped her father crush his enemies in a great victory. She was sent to her promised husband in a well-armed ship along with an honorable company and a great treasure. But her trip was tragic. A violent storm put the ship in danger. The sailors panicked, and trying to save their own lives in a small boat, ran into a quick death. The ship with the women was stranded on the beach of Majorca Island. Luckily, a country gentleman, who happened to pass by with his servant, saw the defenseless women and took them to his castle.

The gentleman and the ladies could not communicate because of the language barrier. He realized that Alatiel was a woman of high rank from the honor and respect she received from the other ladies. She was exceedingly beautiful in spite of the past events. As the days went by, she looked more and more gorgeous. The gentleman fell helplessly in love and decided to marry her, or at least, get her favors. Alatiel rejected all his advances. She understood that she had fallen among Christians and it would be of no help to make herself known. She took counsel from her company, and they all agreed to preserve their chastity. Meanwhile, her lover resolved to use cunning to achieve his goal.

One night he planned a party in her honor and had an extraordinary dinner prepared. He had perceived that she liked wine, something to which she was not accustomed because her religion forbade it. Accordingly, he offered a great variety of drinks and found the best minister of Venus in alcohol. Lured by the taste of wine, she took more than befitted her modesty.

When the guests left, he accompanied her to her bedroom. Unrestrained, the lady undressed before him as she usually did in the presence of her women and went to bed. The ardent lover lost no time, doused the light and followed her. He enjoyed himself immensely, and the lady, until now inexperienced, derived as much happiness. As if repenting her previous denials, now she often invited such pleasant rendezvous, not by words that she didn't know, but by deeds.

The gentleman had a young brother who saw her and was deeply impressed by her unusual beauty. He perceived that he also made an impression on her. In the ensuing days, the only obstacle to carrying out his passion was his brother's presence. One night, he entered his brother's house with some trusted friends and stole the girl away to a ship which had been enlisted for that purpose. There the inflamed man proceeded to comfort her with his fiery sword in such a way that she soon felt at ease with him. Unfortunately, the romance did not last long.

One day Alatiel's new companion was at the ship's stern looking out over the waves. Suddenly, the two ship owners pushed him overboard, and he was lost in the sea. When Alatiel found out, both men tried to soothe the beautiful lady who was lamenting more her bad luck than her lost lover. They kept her company until late. Then they decided to satisfy their passion, but soon came to harsh words as to who should take her to bed first. Unable to reach an agreement, they jumped quickly from words to deeds and grabbed their knives. One fell dead, while the other barely survived. Their kinfolk came to the cabin and would have unloaded their rage on the frightened woman had the wounded man not clarified the situation. When they landed at their destination, Alatiel's beauty became popular throughout the city, and the prince of Morea came to see her. He was highly excited by her beauty and decided to have her as his wife.

Thanks to the new attentions received, her beauty flourished more and more each day. Her fame spread throughout her husband's lands, and the duke of Athens came to visit them. He couldn't bring himself to believe that Alatiel was human. Although they did not know how to communicate, he drank the amorous potion of love from her sight and was assaulted by an irresistible passion. Slowly he plotted a plan with the prince's chamberlain, who stealthily let him and his friend into the bedroom. Alatiel was sleeping.

The prince was standing at the window gazing at the sea to take a little breeze. The duke's friend cautiously accosted him from behind and stabbed him to death. Quickly, he lifted him up and cast him off into a lonely corner of the shore below. Then, they strangled the chamberlain who had plotted his master's ruin and threw him down, too. The drama unfolded without Alatiel's hearing anything. Alone, the duke gently uncovered her. If he liked her dressed, naked she was endlessly more desirable. He went quickly to bed and satisfied the fire of his passion, while the sleeping lady thought him to be the prince. Late in the night, he returned with his household to his dominion. Since he was married, he took Alatiel to a secret resort on the shore and enjoyed her as a mistress.

When the prince's attendants didn't find him, they thought he had gone on some privy excursion. But a few days later they discovered the two dumped bodies and gathered who the author of the heinous crime was. The power of state passed to the late prince's brother, and war was declared to avenge his death. The duke of Athens mustered his forces to defend his dominion and received help from many allies, among them the prince of Constantinople who was his wife's brother. As a matter of fact, the duchess of Athens secretly informed her brother of her husband's infidelity and asked his help to restore her honor in the most proper way.

The duke, forgetting what he had done previously, easily allowed himself to introduce the lady to his brother-in-law, the prince of Constantinople. He, too, received the full impact of her fascination and decided to get her for himself. One day, he left the battle front pretending to be sick, returned alone to Athens, and proposed to the duchess that he would avenge her honor. She believed him and helped arrange Alatiel's kidnapping. Thus the prince of Constantinople, on pretense of helping his sister, was able to satisfy the passion he had carefully concealed from everyone. He took the lady to an island. At first she bemoaned her ill-fated charm, but then she conformed as usual to the new development.

This too, did not last long. The king of the Turks, aware that his enemy, the prince of Constantinople, was on the island honeymooning with this famous mistress, invaded the island by surprise at night, caught Alatiel among the prisoners, and without delay took her as his wife. This new marriage did not last long, for the emperor of Constantinople, eager to avenge his son, sent an ally of his, Bassano, against the king of the Turks. Bassano fought his enemy and won.

During this period of hostilities, Alatiel was taken care of by a courtier who happened to know her language. Happy to find someone with whom she could communicate after so long a time, a new closeness was born between the two, and they easily passed from friendly commerce to amorous intercourse. When they heard of the king's defeat, they fled to Rhodes. There they lived for a short time, but her lover died and she was left under the protection of a friend who was a merchant.

This man had to leave Rhodes, and she agreed to follow him posing as his sister. Later, to prevent some foreseeable inconvenience, they agreed that Alatiel would pass as his wife during the voyage. Accordingly, they were lodged in the same cabin, and what they had not anticipated did indeed occur. The darkness, the small size of the only available bed, and the heat of their bodies, all conspired to warm their blood and make them forget their dead friend.

When they arrived at their destination, by chance she ran into Antigonus, an old aristocrat whom she had known at her father's court. Alatiel recognized him at once. When she had a chance, she approached him.

"Are you Antigonus of Famagosta?" she asked him, blushing.

"Yes, I am," replied the old gentleman. "I have the feeling I know you, but I can't recall where I met you."

Alatiel, assured that it was he, put her arms around his neck and started to cry. With copious tears, she told him her name, and the other was amazed to meet the princess that everybody believed dead at the bottom of the sea.

"I wish I were dead," she replied in tears. "I wouldn't have had the kind of life I have gone through. I feel my father would wish the same thing if he knew about it."

Antigonus consoled her and promised his assistance. After he knew everything about her misfortunes, he gave his wise advice.

"Be glad nobody knew who you were during all this time. Now follow my instructions and you will be restored to your royal status."

Alatiel followed his advice step by step. She was introduced to the king of Cyprus, who sent her to her father, the soldan, with much honor and protection. The whole family was happy to have her back. When the soldan asked why she never gave any news of herself although alive, Alatiel repeated what she had been told to say by old Antigonus.

In short, she said that after the storm she was rescued by some people of authority who took her to a convent of ladies dedicated to God according to their religion. The ladies treated her kindly, and she joined them in serving Saint Go-in-deep, a saint for whom the women of that country have a great devotion. After she learned some of their language, afraid to say the truth to those Christians, she identified herself as the daughter of a gentleman from Cyprus. The abbess of the convent, heedful of her honor, never consented to send her to Cyprus until a group of gentlemen with their wives went there on their way to the holy places. Luckily, she met old Antigonus, who could give more details of the rest.

The soldan was rejoiced beyond measure. When the extraordinary news reached the king to whom she had first been promised as a wife, he was happy to receive her. And Alatiel, the girl who had relations with eight men nearly ten thousand times, was accepted by her husband as a virgin, and she made him believe so.

Hence comes the Italian saying that "A kissed mouth forfeits no luck, but is renewed just like the moon." (*Bocca baciata non perde fortuna, ma si rinnova come la luna.*)

## 18.  Feminine Revenge

When the Roman Empire passed from the French to the German people, constant hostilities erupted between the two nations. The king of France and his son levied a huge army and started a military campaign. The official functions of the country were entrusted to Count Gautier, a widower in his forties, who commanded respect for his virtues and admiration for his distinguished person. Every day he would discuss the handling of his office with the queen and her daughter-in-law, that is, the prince's wife.

It so happened that the princess conceived a deep affection for Count Gautier, which soon turned into a burning passion. Being herself alone, she thought it would be rather easy to seduce a man who had no wife. One day she sent for him and received him in her bedroom. Twice the gentleman asked what he could do for the princess, and both times she gave no answer. Finally, among sighs and tears, she blushed and confessed her passion with a trembling voice. Then she folded her head on his chest, but he professed his loyalty to her husband and rejected her offer.

Immediately, her love changed to a furious rage. She tore her hair and started to yell for help as if she had been attacked. Aware of the danger, Count Gautier ran home, set his two children on horseback, and took refuge in London before he was caught by the police. Unable to capture him, the prince had him and his descendants condemned to perpetual banishment.

Count Gautier changed his and his children's names and lived as a beggar. Luckily a rich young lady coming out of the church asked for his little girl, and Count Gautier gave her away so she might be brought up in the warmth of a sound home. Then he moved away with his son close to another church.

While he was begging, his young son started to mingle with

some children in the neighborhood and played with them. He became a friend of the son of the king's marshal, who requested the poor exile to leave the boy in his house, so both boys could be good friends. Happy that he could place both children in good homes, Count Gautier went to Ireland where he took a lowly job in the service of a country earl.

As the years went by, the daughter grew into a beautiful woman. She kept the secret of her name and position, and her foster mother was planning to give her as a wife to a worker. But things happened otherwise, for the lady's son fell in love with her. Since he thought that she was a woman of low social standing, he wouldn't dare displease his parents by asking to marry her.

The more he tried to repress his love the worse it became. He fell ill and the doctors couldn't determine what his ailment was. Finally, a young physician happened to notice that each time the young lady would come into the sick man's chamber, the beating of his pulse would rise exceedingly high. On the contrary, whenever she left his room, the beating would go down. That circumstance led him to the right diagnosis, and he informed the parents about the young man's repressed passion. The mother asked the girl if she had a lover, but found out that she was a moral lady who would not surrender to anybody except a legitimate husband.

"Come on," pressed the older lady. "Suppose that our king, who is a young man, would ask for your favors, would you deny him?"

"The king may force me," she replied, "but he would get nothing of my free will."

Seeing her decision, the lady told her son that he would have a chance to be alone with the girl after he recovered. Actually, he grew worse and worse until his parents accepted the idea of his marrying a girl of unknown origin.

As to the other child of Count Gautier, he grew up strong and brave, so that he became one of the most valiant knights in the English kingdom. During the bubonic plague, death took the marshal and the whole family with whom he grew up. Only the marshal's daughter survived, who married the young man, and thus raised him to the high dignity of marshal of England.

Eighteen years later, Count Gautier returned to London to find out what had happened to his two abandoned children. He was old and totally changed. First he saw how well his son had fared, so he left unknown to see his daughter. He arrived as a beggar, and one day his son-in-law, without knowing him, told one of his servants to feed the poor man. There he found a group of children who belonged to his daughter.

They all came around the old man and started to fondle him. As if moved by some mysterious virtue, they had sensed him to be their grandfather. The mother came and bade them to return to their governess, but the children insisted on staying with the old man—for he loved them more than their governess. The old man got up to honor the mistress, and she did not recognize him at all. Her husband, who had already grown bored with her, heard that the children would not obey their governess and exclaimed, "Confound them! By their mother they come from a vagrant, and that's what they like." Count Gautier swallowed that affront the same as he had done with many others. In any case, he was offered a humble job at the palace because the children were so fond of him.

At this time it happened that the king of France died and his son ascended to the throne. A new war broke out with Germany, and the king of England went to help the new sovereign of France. Count Gautier went to war, and unknown as he was, kept in touch with his son and son-in-law. Both men were on the battle front, each unaware of the other.

During the campaign, the queen of France fell very ill. Before dying, she confessed her wrong against Count Gautier and asked her confessor and other courtiers to inform her husband of the truth. The king was pleased to hear it and made it publicly known that he restored Count Gautier and his descendants to their noble estate. The proclamation being officially certified, Count Gautier gathered together his son and son-in-law and made himself known. After joyful emotion, the son-in-law was sent to bring the news to the king. Among merriment and tears, the long-suffering count was reinstated in all his fortune and prospered more than ever together with his children's families.

## 19.  Heroic Chaste Wife

A group of Italian merchants, while in Paris, had gathered at a certain inn to spend a night together enjoying each other's company. Discussing different subjects, they came to speak of their wives, whom they had left at home. One of them remarked, "If I have a chance with a pretty girl, I get all the fun I can. After all, whether I believe it or not, my wife does just the same when she has a chance." Other merchants agreed with him. Only one, Bernabo of Genoa, said that he had full confidence in his wife's virtue. She was above all praise and a hundred-percent chaste wife.

"Slow down," rejoined a young man named Ambrose, mocking Bernabo's faith in his wife. "I wonder if you received that privilege above all men from the emperor."

"Not from the emperor," rejoined Bernabo, somewhat bothered, "but from God, who is above the emperor."

"You may believe what you say. Yet, you are not aware of human nature. We spoke a lot of our wives. They are all the same, and yours is no exception. We know better. Listen to me. Man is the noblest animal ever created by God. He is firmer than woman. And in spite of it, he misses no chance to have his own way with a woman he desires. How can a woman, who is less firm, abstain from enjoying a man she likes? Your wife, too, is made of flesh and blood as they all are, and you shouldn't be so dogmatic about her virtue."

"Don't come to me with sophisms," replied Bernabo. "I am no philosopher. I am a merchant, and as such I'll tell you that foolish women do as you say. But good women take care of their honor."

"Indeed," said the other, "if a horn would sprout on their forehead each time they play such games, I believe they would take good care of their honor. Dishonor does not consist in doing the wrong thing, but in being discovered. So, if they feel safe, they do it.

Believe me, the only chaste woman is the one who hasn't been solicited or who has been rejected. I have a little bit of experience and can assure you of this: in a short time I would get from your wife what I have received from others."

"Nonsense," said Bernabo. "If you feel so confident, I bet you my head against a thousand florins of yours."

"What do you want me to do with your head?" replied the young merchant who had grown heated over the discussion. "Why don't you bet five thousand of yours against my thousand? In three months I'll bring you all the proof you need."

The other merchants tried to stop the bargain because they foresaw that nothing good would come of it. But the two merchants were inflamed and sealed their bet.

Ambrose left for Genoa to study all the details concerning Bernabo's wife and found that she was above any suspicion. However, he bribed an old maid to receive her cooperation. The old woman, with the excuse that she had to go elsewhere, asked the honest wife to keep a chest in her custody for three days. Unaware of the trap, she agreed to it. Ambrose was hiding in the chest. He came out during the night while the lady was sleeping with her little daughter and observed the setup of the bedroom, furniture, paintings, and everything else. Then he softly uncovered the lady and saw that she was perfect. Only one mark could he detect. Under her left nipple, she had a mole with a few reddish hairs. He covered her again, not to be tempted to rape her, thus endangering his life with such a stubborn woman. On the second night, he again tried to observe as many details as possible and took some souvenirs from a coffer: a purse, some rings and girdles. On the third day, the chest was taken away by the old accomplice, and Ambrose left for Paris to prove that he had won his bet.

When he described the bedroom and showed the lady's belongings, the incredulous husband told him that he might have gotten them through an unfaithful servant. But when the detail of her body was revealed, he felt a cold knife piercing his heart. He paid his bet and returned home. Actually, he detained himself a few miles away in a resort that he owned. Then he sent his trusted servant with instructions to get his wife. On the way back, the servant was to kill her in a predetermined place.

The servant followed Bernabo's instructions, but did not have the courage to kill the wife. He took her dress and gave her his own garb. Then he left her alone. The woman took refuge in a little town and disguised herself as a sailor. In the harbor, she (he) accepted a job on a ship with a Catalan captain and gained his trust thanks to her (his) good behavior.

In the course of time, the soldan cast his eyes on this sailor and wanted him in his services, where she gained his royal favor. On one occasion the disguised sailor—already a high officer—was sent to a huge market where many Christian merchants would concur. Since she knew the language, she visited several Italian ships. Suddenly her sight was attracted by a purse and a girdle which she recognized to be hers. She asked if they were for sale. The merchant started to laugh. "They are not for sale," he said. "But if you want, you can have them."

"What are you laughing at? Is there anything wrong with an officer inquiring about those items?"

"Sir," replied Ambrose, "I laugh at the way I got them."

"If you haven't any objection, please tell me that story."

Ambrose began his version of the adventure. The good woman understood the chain of events that had conspired against her. She pretended to enjoy the whole joke and arranged some business to keep Ambrose in town until she could contrive a scheme to induce her husband to come to the same place. Poor and neglected, Bernabo came down. One day she induced the soldan to receive both men at the same audience in order to dig out the truth of the whole episode. The soldan complied and asked with severity both sides of the story. Frightened, Ambrose revealed the truth.

"My lord," said the disguised wife, "you can see how the poor lady was victim both of her lover and her husband: the former destroyed her honor with falsehood; the latter destroyed her life for putting his faith on an unknown liar rather than on a wife that he knew much too well. Ironically, such is their love that neither one knows her. My lord, I beg to punish the deceiver and forgive the dupe, for the lady will be here in your presence."

Ambrose, so far, had been afraid that he would be forced to return the five thousand florins he had earned deceitfully. But now he sensed that a greater danger threatened him. They all waited for the lady to come forth. The disguised wife, putting off her masculine voice, fell on her knees before the soldan.

"My lord, I am the unfortunate victim of this traitor. For six years I have lived under a man's disguise away from my home." She spoke with tears and tore her blouse to show her breast and prove her identity. Everybody was amazed, disbelieving. Bernabo begged her pardon and was graciously received as her husband. Ambrose was spread with honey and left at the mercy of flies and wasps that devoured his flesh. His bones, completely white, were left on the same spot to bear testimony of his treachery to those who saw them.

## 20.  A Lovable Pirate

Master Richard was a judge in Pisa, more gifted with legal wit than physical energy. He thought that he could take care of a wife by the same means as he dispatched his studies and made money. So, in his old age, he took a wife who was both young and beautiful. The wedding was magnificent, but at night the poor groom put up such a poor performance that the next day he had to be revived with malmsey and other confections.

From then on, the good judge was able to judge better his own powers and went on teaching his wife how to practice sexual abstinence according to a calendar of holy feasts. It turned out that every day was dedicated to one or more saints in whose reverence husband and wife should abstain from carnal relations. To this he added a list of fasts and vigils for Lent, Ember days, Fridays and Saturdays, and certain seasons of the moon. That irked the poor wife, whom he hardly touched even once a month. The problem became more acute because he was extremely jealous and kept close vigilance lest someone else teach her workdays as diligently as he had only taught holidays.

So went life, until they took a summer vacation in a seashore resort. One day, they went boating in different boats. The judge was in one boat with the fishermen, his beautiful wife in another with the ladies. Having fun, the ladies drifted a few miles away. Suddenly, a well known corsair named Paganin overtook the boat with the ladies and captured the judge's wife.

The corsair was a young single man, so he decided to keep her for himself. She was weeping sorely, and he tried to console her during the whole day with kind words. At night, his calendar being free of fasts and vigils, he consoled her by deeds. By so doing, he received an excellent response, so that, before he reached his destination, the lady had forgotten everything about the judge and his laws.

She was the happiest of women, enjoying her newfound, lustful lover.

After some time, the judge heard where his wife was being kept by her captor and decided to ransom her. He supplied himself with a copious amount of money. When he arrived, he saw and was seen by his wife. She informed the corsair of her husband's arrival and told him that she had a plan of her own. Next day the judge approached the corsair on the street and treated him in a friendly manner, expressing the purpose of his visit. The other pretended he did not know him.

"Actually, I do have a young lady at home," he admitted. "I don't know whether she is your wife or not. If she says she is, that's all right with me. You'll pay what ransom you like. If she says she is not, forget it."

Anxious, the judge followed the corsair to his house. The lady received them warmly, but treated Master Richard with a distant discretion as if she had never seen him before.

"Alas," he thought, "I have changed so much for the sorrow of her loss that she cannot recognize me." Then he said aloud, "Dear, I never suffered so much since I lost you. Don't you see I am your own Master Richard who came to ransom you?"

"Are you speaking to me?" asked the lady, smiling.

"Take a better look. You'll recognize me. I am your Richard, your legitimate husband."

"Sir," rejoined the lady, "I don't think there is too much to see in you. I have never seen you before."

The judge thought she would say so for fear of the corsair, but this one let him talk to the lady in a separate room. Once alone, the old man struck a pathetic note.

"My life, my soul," he started to say, "don't you know any more your Richard, the man who loves you more than his own life? How can it be? Am I so changed?" The lady started to laugh and cut off his words.

"I know well enough you are Master Richard, my legitimate husband. Don't think I suffer from amnesia. I do know you. The trouble is that you don't seem to know me. Worse yet, you don't know women at all. You should be aware that they need something else besides food and clothing, although for shame they don't dare ask for

66

it. You acted as a preacher of sacraments, feasts, and vigils. This corsair knows none of the holidays you so devotedly respected. I would rather live and work with him while young, and leave jubilees and fasts for my old age."

"What do you say, my soul?" said the judge, who was distressed beyond endurance. "Have you lost all respect for your parents' honor? For your own? How can you live in *mortal* sin with a man who will kick you out as soon as he gets tired of your company? Come back to me and I'll satisfy you."

"Never mind my honor or my parents'," rejoined the lady. "And stop talking about *mortar* sin while I'm enjoying my *pestle* game. At last, I feel like a wife. My man grabs and nips and bites me the whole night. You actually treated me as a whore, because you had to study the cycles of the seasons and geometrical quadratures before the planets concurred to couple us. Now you promise to satisfy me! How do you expect to do it? By sheer blows?"

The old judge was crushed. The lady gave a last scornful glance at him and concluded: "Please, go your way. Don't worry that my man will leave me. And if he does, I know how to take care of myself. Don't expect me to come back to you. No matter how much I squeeze you, there is no juice to come out. Now get out or I'll yell that you tried to force me."

The poor man went away defeated. To those who addressed him, he would only answer, "The darned hole will have no holidays." He died before long, and his demise had a quick legal aftermath—the two lovers rushed to legalize their union through marriage.

# THE THIRD DAY

## Satisfied Wishes

## 21. Seduced by Nuns

"I haven't seen you for quite a few years. What have you been doing?" asked Masetto, talking to an old friend of his.

"Working as a gardener in a convent," answered the other.

"How did you like it?" kept on Masetto.

"Awful! Those nuns are a pain in the neck. They never know what they want. I called it quits."

"How is it to live with so many women around?"

"Worse than hell. Imagine eight young women and an abbess. It drives you crazy."

Masetto had a different opinion than his friend. He was young and able-bodied, so he inquired about the town where the convent was and decided to take the job, if it was still available. To be acceptable to the lay administrator, Masetto made like he was a deaf and dumb beggar and asked by signs to be helped. He started to cleave wood, clean the courtyard, and do other needed jobs. The administrator liked him, and a few days later, secured his job permanently from the abbess. The nuns were young and lovely. They were whimsical, and sometimes they would talk freely or mock him, thinking that he couldn't hear them. The abbess didn't make any fuss, supposing perhaps that he was as tailless as he was speechless.

One day, as he was resting on the ground, he overheard two young nuns talking. The more daring of the two was saying that more than once she had felt the desire to lie with the deaf gardener. He was a good choice, for he couldn't talk about it. The other nun was more scrupulous. After all, they had promised their virginity to God. But the first one had her mind set. She had heard from the ladies visiting the convent that she was missing a lot, for there is no more enjoyment for a woman than having to do with a man. The time was favorable since all the other nuns were sleeping at that hot hour. She went to awaken Masetto, who was already set to satisfy

70

the anxious nun, while her friend kept watch. Then, loyally, the first nun changed places with the other, while Masetto played dumb to please her. Before leaving, both nuns wanted one more turn, and each concluded that it was delightful.

This activity continued for some time, until one day they were caught by a nun peeking out of her cell. She called the other nuns, whose first impulse was to denounce the two sisters to the abbess. But they changed their minds and shared the deaf young man among themselves. The abbess was unaware of all this. One day Masetto was sleeping under a tree and the wind had uncovered him. The abbess saw this and fell into the same appetite which had taken hold of her nuns. She aroused the young gardener and took him to her room. There she kept him for several days to the no small displeasure of the other nuns who went to complain that the gardener was neglecting the work in the courtyard. She sent him to work for a while, but was anxious to have him back to enjoy pleasures that she would undoubtedly denounce in others. Poor Masetto was in such demand from all of them that he was becoming physically exhausted. Consequently, one night while with the abbess, he decided to loosen his tongue.

"Madame," he said, "I have heard that one rooster is enough for almost a dozen hens, while a dozen men can hardly satisfy one woman. Now I have to take care of nine. I can't stand it any longer." The lady was amazed to hear him talk, and Masetto justified himself by saying that he was not born dumb, but had lost his speech on account of sickness. She believed it, but was puzzled about his relations with the other nuns. To keep the situation under control they all agreed to share the man in a way that wouldn't disgrace the convent. They spread the good news that Masetto had recovered his speech thanks to their intercession with the saint in whose name their convent had been dedicated.

When the old administrator died, they appointed Masetto in his place and kept enjoying his favors, thus begetting copious monkins and nunnies that they brought up discreetly. It so happened that Masetto, in his old age, returned home rich and a father without having to go through the pains of rearing children.

## 22. The Raped Queen

King Agilulf married Theodolinda, the beautiful widow of his predecessor. One of the stablemen was a handsome man who fell in love with the queen, although he was a man of low social standing. He never let his passion be known. He knew that he might never win her favor, but was secretly happy that he had placed his thoughts so high.

Inflamed by such a fire, he fancied he might replace the king in bed, since he did not enter the queen's bedroom every night. Many times he hid himself in the hall between the king's and queen's bedrooms and espied what the king's attire was and how he behaved. Accordingly, one night he wore a mantle as the king did, and he, too, carried a taper and knocked at the queen's chamber with a wand. A sleepy maid opened the door and took the light. He went to bed and pretended to be troubled to avoid speaking. Then he took the queen in his arms and knew her carnally several times.

After he left, the king felt like visiting the queen for the same purpose and greeted her cheerfully. She felt encouraged by that and said, "My lord, how does it happen that you come back to me after your previous unusual performance? Watch out." The king immediately understood that the queen had been deceived. But he was a wise man and didn't give the immediate answer that a fool would.

"Dear," he said, disguising his true feelings, "don't you think I am man enough to come back for a second serving?"

"Of course, my lord," replied the queen. "I only beg you to take care of your health."

"If it so pleases you, I'll follow your advice," concluded the king and left. He thought it over and inferred that the seducer had to be one of the household. He took a lantern and went to feel the hearts of all the men sleeping in a long hall. Whoever had deceived the

72

queen might still be under the spell of his emotions, and his heart-beats as yet would not be normal.

The stableman was awake, and upon seeing the king, he became terrified. But he saw him without weapons and pretended to be sleeping. The king touched many sleeping people and finally found his man. To keep everything secret, he cut a lock of hair from the suspected man's temple, so he wouldn't miss him the next day. The servant was a shrewd man and understood the king's plan. So he went to clip likewise all the servants' hair.

The next day, the king gathered all of them to pick out the culprit. Upon realizing that he had been thrown off the trail, he avoided a scandal by dismissing them graciously: "He who did it shall not do it again, and all go in peace."

## 23.  Unaware Middleman

A Florentine noblewoman adorned with beauty, physical charms, and engaging manners was married to a wool dealer. She felt the distance in rank and tastes between her husband and herself. That cooled her feelings, and she decided to deny him sexual enjoyment as much as possible. At the same time, for her own satisfaction she wanted to find a gentleman worthier than her merchant husband. She cast her eyes on a discreet man of good station and, little by little, fell in love. The gentleman did not perceive her feelings, while the lady, to avoid further complications, did not dare to send a go-between or any kind of message. She noticed that the man she secretly loved used to visit a certain friar, a simpleton who ranked high in public opinion because of his saintly life. He seemed a good prospect to carry out her scheme.

One day she went to confess with the holy friar. After the ususal ritual, she asked him for special advice. "Father," she said, "you know what a rich man my husband is and how much he loves me. Let me tell you that I love him more than myself and would do nothing to displease his honor and pleasure. A distinguished gentleman, tall and well-dressed, has laid siege on me. He is a good friend of yours and seems to be unaware of my devotion to my husband. Please tell him to leave me in peace. There must be quite a few women who would like to be courted by such a fine man, but I don't want to have any part of it." The holy friar recommended that she practice charity and have faith in his work. She finished her confession and quietly filled his hands with money.

Not too long after, the friar met the gentleman and rebuked him in a civil way for his gallant pressures against the above lady. The gentleman denied everything, but the friar insisted that he knew the whole truth and warned him against making any more advances to the lady. Since he was quicker of wit than the friar, he got wind of the lady's plot. Therefore, he promised he would not meddle any more with her. Then he passed cautiously close to the lady's house and saw her. She showed a gracious and merry countenance upon seeing him and knew that she was likeable to him. In order to excite his interest more, she returned to the friar a few days later and complained again.

"That darned friend of yours," she said, "was born for my despair. He will force me to start a scandal."

"Hasn't he stopped bothering you?" inquired the friar.

"Not at all," she exclaimed in despair. "He has grown even bolder and has dared to send me a purse and some girdles as gifts. I almost lost my patience. I thought I'd send back the gifts with the same messenger, but I was afraid she would keep them herself and make him believe I had accepted them. Please return them to him and make him understand I need none of this trash. If he doesn't stop this nonsense, I'll inform my husband."

She was weeping sorely and threw a rich purse and some elegant girdles on the friar's lap. He gathered those items and gave full assurance that he would take good care of the whole business. Then he warned her not to say anything to anyone, for it would cause great damage to her reputation. She showed herself somewhat consoled and said, "Some nights ago I dreamed of my mother and other relatives who seemed to be in need of special prayers. I recommend their souls to your attention." And she put a purse full of florins in his hands.

The holy man confirmed her devotion with many pious examples and gave her full absolution. Unaware that he was being gulled, he angrily went to reproach his good friend, who faintly denied having sent any gifts. The friar, already incensed, showed the proofs of his accusations. The gentleman pretended he was abashed and took back the purse and girdles. Then he passed by the lady's house and circumspectly showed the items he had received. The lady was gratified to see that her plot was proceeding from good to better.

One day her husband left on a business trip. Immediately she went to complain to the friar that she couldn't stand his friend any longer. She would speak the truth, but she had given her word to the holy man and wouldn't start a scandal before taking his counsel. "Now this devil knows that my husband went to another town for business. This morning at a certain hour he came to my garden and climbed to my bedroom window. I woke up frightened and started to yell. But he mentioned his name and said he was your friend. Naked as I was, I ran to close the window to his face. I have had it!" The friar couldn't believe what he had just heard, but she assured him that she had recognized the gentleman clearly.

"This is the end," admitted the holy man. "Since God has preserved you from shame, give me one more chance to bridle this loose devil. If I succeed, good. If not, do whatever you like."

"All right," answered the lady. "This is the last time I forgive him, and only for your sake."

The friar went to see his friend and gave him a harsh reprimand. The other showed a studied embarrassment and said evasively, "Have I put Christ on the cross?"

"Shame on you!" rebuked the friar. "Have you forgotten what you did this morning? Where were you before daylight?"

"I don't know, but whatever it was, the news came to you too soon."

"Here is a gentleman," exclaimed the holy man, "an honorable man who climbs to the chaste lady's window..."

At the end of a long sermon, the gentleman had gathered all the information he needed. Early in the morning, he climbed the tree and jumped into the lady's bedroom. She was waiting impatiently and received him in her arms, thankful to the friar for teaching him the way.

## 24. The Road to Holiness

An honest and rich man called Puccio was a devout believer who had become a tertiary of the Franciscan Order. He had a young wife and a maid. Since he had enough to lead a comfortable life, he did not work. Being a simple chap, he spent his time saying prayers, hearing mass, and chanting holy hymns. His wife was less than thirty years old, fresh and beautiful. Because of her husband's devotion, she was fasting more than she wished. At night, when she would have liked to have fun, he would tell her of the life of Christ, the preaching of Friar Nastagio, the complaint of Mary Magdalene, or the like.

One day a young monk came from Paris. He was a nice person, a witty talker, and a keen scholar. He became friendly with Puccio who invited him frequently to his home. The monk was honored by Puccio's wife. He saw she was fresh and plump and guessed what it was that she lacked most. He therefore thought he would give her a good supply and save her holy husband a lot of trouble. Subtly, he tried to inspire his desire in her and, on the first available occasion, made a discreet request. The lady did not make too many objections, except for the fact that her husband was always at home. The young monk, aware of this obstacle, devised a plan of his own. One night he put it into action.

"Puccio," he said, "I understand the thing you want most is to become a saint. You are going about it all wrong. There is a shorter way. Neither the pope nor the great prelates want this way to be known for one simple reason. The clergy live by alms and charities. If people knew the short way to saintliness, the clergy's income would diminish. Since you are a friend, I'll tell you. But not a word of it to anybody."

The devout tertiary became eager to find out and promised to keep it secret. The monk explained that all Puccio's past sins would be purified if he followed the prescribed penance, and his future sins would pass away with the holy water. He had to do a general and diligent confession of all his sins and a forty-day fast during which he should abstain from touching any woman, including his own wife. Moreover, at night, he should have a plank set in such a way that he could lean against it and keep rigid while watching the sky with stretched arms in imitation of a crucifix. There he should stay motionless until dawn, reciting hundreds of prayers in remembrance of the passion of Christ who died on the cross. After a few hours of sleep in the morning, a new diet of prayers, masses and orisons should follow. "If you perform the scheduled acts of compunction," concluded the young monk, "you will have a feeling of eternal beatitude before the end of the whole devotion."

"Oh!" exclaimed the pious man. "That isn't hard to do!" His wife heard of it and thought that the device was excellent. To help, she said she would fast with him during the day. But, at night, when the charming monk came to see her in secret, he would bring a good meal, which they would enjoy while the poor husband was engaged in his holy exercises. Then the two lovers would spend the night in bed together.

It so happened that their bedroom was separated from the place where the saintly man was standing crosswise by only a thin wall. One night the two lovers loved too well, and the husband felt the floor shake. He completed a series of one hundred paternosters and inquired about the noise. The wife, who was astride between Saint Benedict's and Saint John Gualberto's beasts, tried to repress her delight and answered, "I am restless."

"Restless for what?" asked he.

"I'll tell you why," replied the merry woman. "I have heard you repeat the old saying, 'Who suppeth not by night must toss till morning light.'"

"I told you not to fast," said the pious man. "Now try to rest and don't move around with such jolts."

"Don't worry," she told him. "Do the best you can for yourself as I try for myself." Puccio, reassured, kept on counting his prayers. The two lovers moved to a different bedroom and pursued earthly delight along a parallel road that took the pious husband to heavenly bliss.

## 25.  A Wife for a Horse

Master Francesco, a gentleman from Pistoja, was very wealthy and intelligent, but had the flaw of great greed. His wife was an exceedingly lovely lady and very virtuous. One day, he was appointed for a six-month period as provost in Milan and desired to have the most appealing horse to take his trip to that town.

It so happened that Richard, a young and rich man, had the most admirable horse in town. Master Francesco knew that Richard had been courting his lovely and prudent wife in vain. Covetous as he was, he asked Richard to sell him the steed, hoping to receive it as a gift. The young lover answered that he wouldn't sell his horse for all the gold in the world. He would rather give it to Master Francesco on condition that he let him have a secluded interview with his wife. The greedy husband accepted the deal, hoping to outwit the idealistic lover. He went to his wife and explained his good luck. The lady was displeased at being involved in the deal, but he forced her to promise she would not open her mouth, no matter what Richard proposed.

The interview was arranged, and Richard exposed his long love and great admiration for the lady. His words were sincere and had more effect than all the courting he had uselessly done before. "Madame," he said, "I shall always be happy to do whatever you wish. Without your love, my youth will fade away. May your kindness be equal to your past rigor. Don't be as harsh as before, or you will cause my death and carry the guilt for the rest of your life."

Such arguments seemed to move the discreet lady, but she could hardly repress her sighs, while subtle flashes of comprehension sprang from her eyes. After a long pause he understood the husband's trick, but he was encouraged by the lady's reaction and decided to give himself the answer that he had hoped to receive from her.

"Dear Richard," he said with a sharp feminine voice, "although I have had tokens of your love for a long time, I don't want you to believe that my heart is as rigid as my countenance. I must defend my reputation. But do not keep your hopes high. After my husband leaves for Milan, I may make a favorable decision on your behalf. I only promise this: If you see two towels displayed at the window of my bedroom, it means that I shall be waiting for you to come to a secret meeting."

After he spoke for the lady, he took his normal tone of voice and thanked her with deep gratitude and gave full assurance that he would follow her advice. He got up and went to Master Francesco who was waiting for the result of the interview far away in a conspicuous place in the house. Richard addressed him with sour frustration. "Sir," he said, "you promised to let me talk to your wife, not to a statue!" The other, delighted by those words, requested the horse. Richard was resigned and stuck to the deal.

A few days later, Master Francesco left for Milan. His wife considered the long term of loneliness in the months ahead and the generous nature of her young lover. Then she took two little towels and hung them from the bedroom window.

## 26. A Jealous Wife

In Naples, one of the most amusing and intriguing towns in Italy, there was a noble and well-known gentleman named Richard Minutolo. He had a lovely wife, yet he fell in love with another lady who was considered the most beautiful woman in town. She was named Catella. He tried in vain to get her attention. An exceedingly jealous woman, she was so much in love with her husband that there was no way to turn her from her steadfastness. Richard suffered true depression, but finally took counsel to change his plan. He chose another lady to prove that his ill-chosen love was healed and began a show of jousting and tourneying for her as he had done for the previous lady. After a certain time, even Catella was convinced that Richard had lost every trace of love for her.

One day, they met on the beach with a group of friends and spoke with a degree of familiarity that they had never had before. At the first chance, Richard hinted that Catella's husband had a secret love. The jealous woman strenuously pursued the matter. After lengthy entreaties and due oath, Richard confided that her husband had only pretended to overlook the past—he was now trying to get even by courting his rival's wife.

"Under my advice," he kept saying, "my wife gave him hope and finally promised to meet him in a public bathing place. Things have gone pretty far with your husband, and I thought I should inform you, for he required your absolute fidelity when I was madly in love with you. To prove that all this is true, the date is fixed for tomorrow at noon. I'll not send my wife. But if I were you, I'd go and surprise him and afterwards shame him for the affront he would do to us both."

The more they talked, the more Catella fell into Richard's trap. When she returned home, she started to observe every move her

81

husband made. The innocent man was absorbed by other preoccupations. This aroused her suspicions ever more, and she spent the whole night thinking what she would tell him when she caught him red-handed.

At noon, she went to the public bathing place. Richard had arranged everything with an old lady who took care of the place. He went to rest in a dark room. Upon her arrival, he got up and, whispering, started to kiss and embrace her. Then they went to bed, both avoiding speech because both wanted to hide their identities. Richard enjoyed the interlude more than Catella. Finally, she broke out with rage. "How sad is a woman's lot! I have loved you faithfully for eight years and now I find you are aflame with passion for another woman. Disloyal traitor! Who do you think I am? Catella! Yes, Catella, the woman you have cheated! Disloyal dog! You have lavished me with more caresses in one afternoon than the rest of our married life! At home you play tired and undone, but you are fine with other outlets."

Richard enjoyed her words and again started to kiss and pet her. The lady became more enraged. "You won't fool me," she said. "I will never forgive you for this affront. What does Richard's wife have that I don't? Don't touch me!!! I'll revenge this!"

After listening to a long string of complaints and reproaches, Richard, holding her tight in his arms, decided to reveal the truth in order to prevent some other complications. Catella, deluded, tried to free herself. She would have yelled, but he stopped her from doing so.

Then he started to sweeten her fury. Nothing good would come of a scandal. First of all, he wouldn't admit the facts but would say that she went to the secret meeting for money and now was enraged because she did not get as much as she had expected. People are more inclined to believe bad intentions than good purposes, and he would be believed more easily than she. There was also a second reason to keep in mind. Mortal hate would arise between him and her husband, and either one or both might lose their lives. In any event, she would not be happy with the tragic result.

"After all," he concluded, "you are not the first woman, nor will you be the last, to be deceived for love. I didn't do it to take anything away from you, but out of the great love that I have always felt for you."

"Richard," she said with sadness, "my good faith and jealousy have brought me here. You have what you wanted. Now leave me alone, and I hope God will avenge the abuse I have received."

Richard was gratified by her reaction, but didn't release her. With sweet words and affectionate sighs, he did his utmost to be pardoned and gain her understanding. Human and sensitive as she was, she didn't miss that a lover's kisses taste sweeter than those of a husband.

## 27.  The Lover's Return

Ted Elisei, a noble young man from Florence, had enjoyed the love of Madame Ermellina, the wife of a rich merchant. One day, without any explanation, she suddenly refused to receive him. The young man, seeing that there was no hope to get her back, was affected by a strange spell of melancholy and finally decided to withdraw from the world. He took an assumed name, associated himself with a merchant, and became wealthy.

Seven years later, while singing a tune he had composed for Madame Ermellina, he felt homesick and eager to see her again. He wore a pilgrim's attire and went back to Florence incognito. During the day, he saw Ermellina's house all locked up and felt a strange foreboding. Then he sought out his brothers and sisters and heard some tragic news. They were mourning Ted's death, his body having been discovered a few days before. Ermellina's husband was arrested because of rumors concerning her relations with the young man and was convicted on the basis of circumstancial evidence. Ted was surprised to find out that everybody thought him dead.

At night, in his bedroom he could not close his eyes. Late that night, he saw three men join a lady. He espied them eagerly and heard that they were happy that Ted Elisei's murder had been blamed on somebody else. They pledged to keep their secret forever, otherwise they would be in danger.

The next day, Ted went to visit Madame Ermellina and found her seated on the ground, full of tears and sorrow. With pangs of compassion, he greeted her and promised that her grief would be turned to joy in the next twenty-four hours. By talking, he showed that he knew many details of her life, and the lady believed him to be a saintly prophet. Ted, garbed as a pilgrim, accepted that role and told her that God had allowed all that to happen because she had committed a great wrong to her lover of old.

The lady knew that some rumors had been whispered by a friend of the late Ted Elisei the day his body was discovered. Yet, she was amazed at the pilgrim's detailed knowledge and regretted her harsh rejection of a lover whose image had never been dispelled from her heart. The pilgrim inquired the reason of her abrupt refusal and found that she had been frightened by the threats of a friar who learned of her secret love through a confession.

"Madame," stated the pilgrim, "this is the only cause of all your trouble. First of all, there was no reason for you to break your lover's faith in such a rude manner. You caused him to live unhappily in a long period of exile, and the Lord is punishing you. As to the friar, I am a friar myself, as you can see. Let me tell you that in old times friars and monks sacrificed themselves for the good of mankind. Now they go not only after laywomen, but also after nuns. Afterwards they yell louder than others from the pulpit." That he said and many other arguments against false friars. The lady acknowledged her fault, but felt sorry that her repentance was too late because Ted Elisei was already dead.

"Ted is alive," replied the pilgrim. "He only misses your favors."

"Not so," rejoined Madame Ermellina. "I saw him killed before my door and washed his face with my tears, giving occasion to some improper remarks." The pilgrim took off a ring that Ermellina had given him the last night they had been together, and she recognized it. Then he took off the pilgrim's cloth and asked with a Florentine accent: "Do you know me?"

The lady thought he was a ghost and wanted to flee. But Ted reassured her, and she threw herself weeping on his neck. After a happy meeting, Ted again wore his garb and went to inform the police of his discovery. While the officers were taking care of the case, he went to see Ermellina's husband in jail. The assumed murderer was impressed by the strange pilgrim and promised that he would forgive Ted's brothers for having him arraigned, provided that he could escape the gallows.

The next day Ermellina's husband was released, and the pilgrim did his utmost to pacify him with Ted Elisei's brothers and sisters. They were all convinced that their brother Ted was the dead man found at Ermellina's door and wore mourning clothes. A rich banquet was offered by Ermellina's husband to dispel any suspicion and reweld the old friendship with the Elisei family.

85

During the gathering, everyone tried to be generous and nice, but they felt that Ted's kinfolk were missing their late brother. Some of them dared blame the pilgrim for his idea to have such a reconciliation banquet. He thought the time was ripe to remove his disguise and rose to speak. "Nothing is missing from this joyful party except Ted himself. Now I'll reveal him to you." And he cast off his pilgrim's attire and showed his true identity. They were all amazed to hear his story. Then they went to kiss and embrace him as if he had come back from the dead. Only Madame Ermellina refrained from doing so.

"What's that?" inquired her husband. "Why don't you welcome Ted as the other ladies do?"

"Nobody is more thankful than me," answered the lady. "I owe him your freedom and our happiness. You heard some rumors when I mourned Ted's supposed death, and that inhibits me."

"Come now," rejoined the husband. "Do you think I believed those gossips?" The lady went to greet Ted as the other ladies had, and from then on, they kept their relationship alive under discreet cover. Still some doubt was lingering about Ted's true identity because nobody could explain the body that looked exactly like him.

One day a group of soldiers came to greet him: "Good morning, Faziuolo." Ted, who was with his brothers, answered, "You are wrong. I am not Faziuolo." The others, upon hearing him speak, recognized their mistake and added that he resembled exactly a friend of theirs who had come to Florence some time ago, and since then they had lost sight of him. Ted's older brother inquired about Faziuolo's clothing and other tokens, whereby they discovered the identity of the victim they had mistaken for their own brother. Meanwhile, both lovers enjoyed their relationship without any argument.

## 28.   A Drunkard in Purgatory

A holy man—holy, that is, except in matters of women—was made abbot of a convent in Tuscany. A young and lovely woman came to confess to him. He knew her and had been brooding a strong passion for her. It was a pleasure for him to hear that she was the unhappiest wife in the world because her husband was a block-head and, moreover, a very jealous man. She needed help and counsel. And excellent counsel she received indeed.

"Daughter," said the abbot, "I can give you the right remedy, provided that it be kept very secret."

"Don't worry about that. Help me, and nobody will hear about it."

"Your husband must go to purgatory and be purified of his jealousy. He must die first, and then be brought back to life."

"As long as there is no danger to my freedom, please do it," begged the unhappy wife.

"No danger at all," answered the abbot. "What shall I get for such a service?"

"Whatever you like," promised the lady. Then she thought a little and asked, "What can a woman like me do for you?"

"More than I can do for you. Save my life. Give me your love, because I am in love with you," said the monk abruptly.

"I thought you were a saintly man! Is it proper for you to make such a proposition to a lady who comes to ask for advice?"

"My dear," replied the abbot, "holiness is rooted in the soul, but what I request abides in the body. Be proud that your beauty can charm sanctity. After all, I am a man, too, and while your husband is in purgatory, I'll keep you company." Then he added wilily, "I have some jewels, and I wish no other woman to get them but you."

She was hesitant. The abbot perceived this and started to besiege her with more arguments until she was persuaded. But she said she would not comply until her husband was in purgatory. He gave her a ring and promised to take care of her case.

He met the jealous husband a few days later and gave him a glass of wine with a mysterious drug that he had gotten in the Far East. Then he took him to talk with other monks and soon the powder started to work. The man fell on the floor senseless, and they all thought he was dead. The wife came with all the relatives and buried him according to the local customs.

At night, the abbot removed him from the tomb and locked him in a dark cell with the help of a trusted confidant. When he came to his senses and heard that he was dead, the poor man was distressed. Nothing could be seen in the dark. The abbot's confidant gave him some meat saying that his widow had sent it to him. He felt happy, but when he tasted the wine, he cursed her because it was not a good one. After dinner, the monk gave him a good amount of blows, saying it was his penance for his past jealousy. At night, he would go to entertain the assumed widow.

This continued until the lady became pregnant. Immediately, the abbot went to the dark cell, altered his voice, and announced to the husband in purgatory that he would be allowed to return to life. "The prayers of your wife and the abbot have made it possible. Besides, you will beget a child, whom you will devote to Saint Benedict." The man drank his wine. Since it was the same drug, he again fell into a catalepsy and was taken back to the tomb.

The next morning, when he returned to his senses, he saw a small light from a crevice in the tomb and started to yell for help. The monks were stirred with awe and called for the abbot. "Don't be afraid," he warned them. "Take the cross and the holy water and follow me, so we may comply with God's will."

When the buried man saw them, he fell at the abbot's feet and explained what he had been told was the will of God. The sanctity of the abbot grew higher and the stocks of the convent went up. The lady delivered the child on time to the satisfaction of public opinion, and the legal father was happy to call him Benedict after the saint who had interceded for his grace in purgatory.

## 29.  The Estranged Wife

Young Bertrand, the son of Count Isnard of Roussillon, was brought up with other children of the same age, among whom was Gilette, the daughter of a famous physician. At the death of the old count, Bertrand moved to Paris and was put in the king's service. Gilette, who had developed a strong love for the young count, was very sad at his departure. After her father's death she received a rich dowry, but would not accept any suitor's proposal because her love for Bertrand grew stronger and stronger.

One day, she heard that the king was sick with a fistula in his chest which no physician was able to heal. Since she had learned a great deal of medicine from her late father, she gathered an idea of the sickness from its description and decided to take care of it. She went to Paris and by chance met her beloved Bertrand, but he, aware of his high social standing, pretended not to recognize her. The lady was received by the king and promised to heal him in a few days. Although unconvinced, the king had no alternative but to give her a chance—the greatest of doctors had not been able to cure the malady. Then he asked what payment she expected in case she should succeed.

"Majesty," said the young woman, "I shall be pleased to be married by you to a nobleman that I shall request, excepting any royal-blooded prince."

He promised to give her any gentleman she requested as a husband, and in a few days he had to keep his word because Gilette had restored his health. When the king heard of her great love for Bertrand, he was rather amazed. Yet he had to keep his word. The worst reaction came from Bertrand when he was informed of the whole matter. How could he accept a commoner as a wife? The king convinced him to cooperate, and the marriage was celebrated in a splendid fashion.

Gilette married the man she loved more than herself, but Bertrand refused to consummate their marriage until he went back to his estate. He left, and left for good. Instead of going back to his county, he reached Florence and enlisted as an army officer. His untouched wife went back to their county and was received as the legitimate leader by the count's people. She administered the county's business with discretion and wisdom, thus earning the love and allegiance of her subjects. Then she sent two knights to her husband, asking him to return to his estate.

He received the messengers unkindly. "Tell her," said the count indignantly, "that I'll go back under two conditions. First, she must be able to get hold of this ring on my finger. Second, she must become pregnant by me. And now, out of the way—you and your fair lady!"

The poor wife was deeply afflicted by such a stubborn decision. She gathered all her vassals and, after taking counsel with them, notified them that she would take a large amount of money and go throughout the world with her maid to make pilgrimages and work for charity. While they were expressing their regrets, she dressed herself as a pilgrim and left. She went to Florence and lodged in the house of a decent woman, hoping to get news of her husband. Soon she saw him pass by and recognized him. But she feigned not knowing him and asked the hostess who he was. The other lady informed her that he was a stranger who called himself Count Bertrand, a man much loved in Florence. He had fallen in love with a virtuous, but poor, damsel. He had tried hard to obtain her favors, but her mother had prevented their illicit union.

Gilette took note of every detail and prepared her plan. She went to see the mother of the girl her husband loved and asked for her cooperation under oath. When the old lady heard that Gilette would offer a large sum of money as a dowry for her beautiful daughter, she went along with her plan. Her daughter was supposed to go to bed with Count Bertrand in all secrecy, provided he would send her his beautiful ring. In the dark, the girl would be replaced by Gilette, who was also a virgin. Although it was a daring plan, the old lady cooperated.

First of all, the estranged wife received the count's ring, although he was reluctant to give it away. He could not resist the prick of his passion and went to secretly meet his beloved girl. But in the dark he possessed his own wife, who became, to God's will, pregnant. The old lady arranged many meetings without the count's realizing the replacement. At the end, he always left her jewels, and she treasured them.

When Gilette was sure of her pregnancy, she decided to stop the strange game and give a reward to the old lady, who asked for a hundred golden pounds to marry off her daughter. The countess gave her five hundred and many jewels. Then the old lady left the town together with her daughter. The count returned to his lands upon the request of his vassals. Gilette remained in Florence and delivered two beautiful twin boys who resembled their father exactly. After a time she went back to her husband's county, again dressed as a pilgrim.

One day when the count gave a big feast, she took the two boys in her arms and went to the palace. In the presence of all the guests, she knelt in front of her husband and said, "My lord, I am your unhappy wife. I have long wandered around the world. Now keep the promise you made to the two messengers and receive me as your wife."

The count, confused, recognized the ring and his two children and was amazed at her faithfulness. He kissed her tenderly, had her dressed as a countess, and received her as his honored spouse.

## 30. The Devil's Burial

Perhaps you have never heard how the devil can be put back in hell. It may be worthwhile learning about it to save one's soul and to prove that love doesn't exist only in happy homes and palaces, but also in rugged mountains and desert caverns.

It happened long ago in Barbary before its people converted to Christianity. Abilech was the teenage daughter of a rich merchant. Her imagination was captured by the talk of some Christian people who extolled the delight of serving God. She asked the best way to serve God, and they told her it was to eschew worldly things and seclude oneself as hermits do in the deserts of Thebaid.

The girl, carried by an idealistic impulse so characteristic of her age, ran away from her home and went to the desert of Thebaid. After no little toil and sacrifice, she reached the humble hut of a very ascetic hermit and expressed her will to serve God. The holy man saw that she was beautiful and feared a secret desire to succumb to the devil's temptations. He gave her some fruit to eat and recommended that she go to the cell of another hermit in the vicinity, for he was a much better master in holy matters.

She went according to his instructions and met Rusticus, a young hermit, a very devout and pious man. When he learned of her determination to serve God, he decided to keep her in his cell sharing his life of sacrifices. Moreover, he would prove to himself that he could master his carnal appetite and strengthen his ascetic perseverance. Unlikely, during the night he was assailed by many temptations and, finally, confessed himself beaten.

After he made sure through many hints that the girl was totally inexperienced in matters of love and sex, he started to emphasize that the devil was the greatest enemy of God and gave her to understand that the most acceptable service in the eyes of the Lord was to put the devil back in hell. Abilech became eager to do God's pleasure

92

and asked how this could be done. Rusticus stripped off all his clothes and told the girl to do the same. Once naked, he fell on his knees in the act of praying and told her to do the same in front of him. In this position he was inflammed by his passion so that the resurrection of the flesh suddenly took place. Abilech was amazed.

"What is that protruding thing which I do not have myself?" asked the innocent teenager.

"My daughter," he replied, "that is the devil I have been talking about. He is so annoying that I can hardly stand it."

"God be praised!" said she. "I feel better than you because I have none of that devil."

"True, but you have another thing instead of it," replied he.

"What is that?"

"You have hell," affirmed Rusticus. "I feel God sent you here to take this devil away from me. If you allow me to put this devil in your hell, you'll give me great delight and will do a great service to the Lord." Abilech was more than happy to comply with his wish, and the hermit immediately showed her how to jail that cursed devil. Since it was the first time, she felt some pain.

"Truly," she remarked, "that devil is a bad thing and a true enemy of God. Even hell feels bad when he is locked in."

"It will not always happen so," he said to reassure her. To this end, they put the devil into hell six times and succeeded in taking the conceit out of his head. In the ensuing days the devil came back quite often, and Abilech willingly helped the hermit to take him away. This sport pleased her more each day.

In time, Rusticus, who lived on roots and water, could not satisfy her wishes any more and told her that many devils were needed to appease her hell. At times he would respond to her calls, but so seldom did it occur that it was like throwing a bean into a lion's mouth. No wonder the young woman complained that she did not serve God as much as she wished.

While this debate between her growing desire and his weakening powers went on, a fire burned Abilech's house and killed her family. A young man who heard that Abilech had run away from home many months before the fire decided to search for her. He was lucky to find her before the court laid hands upon her inheritance, and he arranged to marry her. During the engagement, some ladies asked Abilech what she had done in the desert to serve God. She told them that she had served God by putting the devil in hell and was sorry she had been taken away from such a pious exercise. When she explained with words and gestures how she had done it, the ladies had a big laugh and told her to have no concern, for her future husband would take care of it, too, because the same thing is done everywhere.

The story went around, and it became a current saying that the best way to serve God is to put the devil back into hell.

# THE FOURTH DAY

Tragic Love Stories

# 31. The Princess's Lover

Prince Tancredi, lord of Salerno, had an only daughter whom he loved more than himself. She married the son of the duke of Capua, but was left a widow after a very short time. She returned home to her father, who received her with affectionate care. But for all his love, he forgot she was still young and needed a husband.

The lady, ashamed to remind her father of this situation, saw many men at her father's court and cast her eyes on Guiscardo, a handsome man of noble manners who was of humble origin. Her love grew more intense each day, and the handsome esquire returned the same feeling towards the young widow.

Determined to get out alone, she discovered a blocked door in her bedroom. She succeeded in opening it to find a rocky cave with a little opening from which some light was coming. She wrote a note explaining her discovery to Guiscardo. Then she placed the note in the hollow of a cane and gave it to him.

"Tonight," she said jestingly to him, "use this as bellows to blow into the fire."

The young man had an idea that there was a hidden meaning in her words and discovered her message in the cane. Then he took a strong rope and went down to the grotto from the top of the hill where the opening was. The lady received him in her chamber and gave him instructions on how they would carry out their secret love affair.

Things went on undetected for some time. One day, Prince Tancredi went to see his daughter in her bedroom to chat with her as usual. The lady was with her women in the garden, so her father sat down on a floor cushion waiting for her to finish with her diversion. Since he was tired, he fell asleep.

When the daughter came back, she did not perceive his presence in the chamber. She left her women outside, pretending that she was going to rest, and shut the outside door. Then she opened the secret door behind which Guiscardo was waiting for her. Both lovers went to bed and, in their merry fun, they awoke Tancredi.

He would have cried aloud at what he saw, but mastered his feelings and decided to be more tactful and thus bring less shame to himself. Guiscardo left from the secret door, and the prince found a way to disappear unseen. Grieved, he had the young man arrested and, weeping, blamed him for the shame he had done to his flesh and blood in return for kindnesses received. Guiscardo only answered, "Love can do more than you or I."

Then he went to see his daughter and, with more tears and sorrow, expressed his deep disillusion. How could she forfeit her virtue and honor with a man of low rank such as was Guiscardo? The guilty man was under custody, but what could the father do against his own daughter? His mind was split between fatherly love inclined to forgive and a just wrath resolved to punish. After he spoke his mind, he started to cry like a child.

The daughter understood that she had been discovered and felt sorry for her lover's danger. She kept calm and avoided any excess of emotional weakness. She admitted her love for Guiscardo and stressed that he only lacked riches, not nobility. Her own father had praised him quite often before discovering their relationship. The fact that she engaged in a secret affair with him proved how insensitive the father was to the legitimate needs of a young woman who had already experienced the delights of the flesh.

The prince left her room, misunderstanding the greatness of her soul. He ordered Guiscardo strangled and his heart brought to his daughter in a golden vase. The lady, suspecting that her father might go to extremes, had prepared a poisonous potion. When she received the golden vase with her lover's heart, she admitted that her father had done right to place it in a befitting container, and took her potion. Informed, the prince ran to her bedroom in despair. The dying daughter asked him not to cry. She wanted a last grace—that her body be buried close to Guiscardo. After a painful wake, the prince gave both lovers an honorable burial in the same site.

## 32. The Angel's Lover

It seems true that hidden flaws do not mar one's virtue. A good reputation often stands on the ability to hide one's defects. A rascal from Imola lived such a wicked life that no one would trust or believe him even when he told the truth. He decided to change. He moved to Venice and became a Minorite friar under the name of Brother Albert. Proceeding with caution and hypocrisy, he made such a show of virtue and sanctity that he became a trustee for many people who wanted to make their wills and a religious counselor for many believers in town. He was consecrated a priest and would shed warm tears every day for the sacrifice of Christ as if it were happening in front of his eyes.

One day a lady came to him for confession. He was glad to take care of her. At the end, he asked whether she had a lover, and she answered with such conceit that Brother Albert told her it was sheer vanity. The lady insisted that her beauty was heavenly and that no man was worthy enough to enjoy it. Tired of hearing her litany of self-compliments, he absolved her and decided to take care of her conceit.

A few days later, he went to see the lady together with a trusted brother from the convent, drew her into a separate room, and fell on his knees before her. Then he started to ask pardon for what he had said during the confession. He needed her pardon desperately, for he had received a divine vision. An angelical man had appeared to him and had given him many harsh blows because he had doubted her divine beauty. That sublime being was in love with her.

"And who was he?" asked the vain lady, enjoying each word he was uttering.

"The Angel Gabriel. He told me he would come back to give me a tough drubbing if you do not forgive me. Besides, he gave me another message for you."

"I told you my beauty was heavenly," rejoined the dim-witted lady, exceedingly pleased. "I do forgive you, and now tell me the other words of the Angel."

"I'll tell you, but the Angel Gabriel bids you to keep it very secret. He is in love with you and many times has tried to keep you company during the night. But he is afraid it might frighten you. He would like to see you, but if he comes as an angel, you cannot touch him. It would be best for him to take a human body. If you agree, he will do so, and you will be the most blessed among living women."

Mrs. Vanity accepted the proposal. She loved the angel, too, and promised to keep secret the fact that such a celestial being would desert the Blessed Mother Mary for her love. Since her husband was absent on a long business trip, it was merely up to the Angel Gabriel to choose the form in which he wanted to visit her.

"You speak wisely," approved the friar. "Now do me a favor that won't cost you anything. Allow the angel to use my body when he comes to visit you. My soul will stay in heaven all the time he spends with you, and this will be a great reward." She agreed and promised to arrange a warm reception for her divine lover.

That night, Brother Albert rode a horse to the house of a lady he trusted and took along his closest friend. There he disguised himself as an angel and went to see the anxious woman, who was waiting with such excitement that her hips didn't touch her slip. When she saw Brother Albert's body in such celestial attire, she fell on her knees. The angel blessed her and carried her to bed. Since she was fresh and dainty, he gave her a better serving than was ever done by her husband, which made her happy beyond measure. Then he returned to his comrade who had kept good company with the lady of the house.

The next day, the woman came to see Brother Albert and repeated the marvelous words she had heard from the loving angel, besides many others that she had invented.

"My lady," said the friar, "my soul was among so many flowers until dawn and I lived in the most delightful place. As to my body, I don't know what happened to it."

"I'll tell you," replied the lady. "It was in my arms the whole night. And if you don't believe me, look under your breast. There you'll find the mark of a long kiss that will last for quite a while."

The affair went on for many nights. One day the vain woman

could not refrain from telling a girl friend that her beauty was such that the Angel Gabriel was in love with her. The other felt like laughing, but pretended to take her seriously. "I wouldn't have believed that angels did such things," commented she.

"Oh, yes!" rectified Mrs. Conceit. "The angel did better than my husband and assured me that they do it above, too."

The gossip went around the town and reached the ears of the lady's in-laws. They decided to set a trap to catch the angel and see if he could fly. Brother Albert heard the gossip and one night went to reproach the lady. But her brothers-in-law were in ambush and broke into the house. The angel was naked and found only one escape. He opened the window and jumped into the canal. By swimming, he reached the house of a poor man and asked that he help him get out of his naked predicament.

The lady's relatives were baffled. They said harsh words and went back to their homes with the angel's belongings. The next day, the poor man who had given refuge to Brother Albert heard the news of the angel's ill-fated visit and dug the truth out of him. Then he blackmailed the unfortunate lover for fifty ducats and told him that on that very day there was to be a festival. Many people would disguise themselves as bears or savages. If he wanted to avoid the lady's kinfolk, the best thing would be for him to wear a disguise and go back to his convent. The sad lover accepted the deal and wore wild clothes and a savage mask. The other man spread the news that people could see the nightly angel at Saint Mark's.

The next day when the place was full of spectators, he removed the mask off the friar's face and said, "Here you have the Angel Gabriel who comes down from heaven to console the Venetian ladies." Exposed to a scornful mob, the unfortunate man was rescued by his brethren, who locked him in his cell for permanent confinement.

## 33.  Love and Crime

A rich man from Marseilles had three daughters. While he was in Spain on a business trip, his oldest daughter, Ninette by name, fell in love with a poor young man of noble birth. The two lovers contrived a way to carry on their affair without being detected. The other two sisters were loved by two rich men, and Ninette's boyfriend, properly instructed by her, approached both of them and put them in touch with their sweethearts.

One day Ninette's lover conceived a bold plan. The three sisters and the three young men should take as much money as possible from their parents and run away. The three couples could live happily wherever they pleased. And so they did. At the end of their itinerary, the six young people bought a rich estate in Crete and lived lavishly.

After some time Ninette's lover, the first to fall in love, grew cold toward her. She was a jealous woman and started to harass his passion for another woman. When she was convinced that she had been betrayed, she made arrangements with an old lady and bought a powerful potion that killed her lover immediately. She mourned his death together with the other members of the group, and her crime remained a secret until the old woman who had prepared the poison was arrested for some other crime. Under torture, she confessed all her misdeeds and the duke of Crete arrested Ninette and received an easy confession.

Magdalene, one of the three sisters, was a very beautiful woman, who had long been courted by the duke, but she had never accepted his propositions. Now that her sister Ninette was in danger, she sent a trusted messenger to let him know that she was at his orders, provided discretion was maintained. The duke was gratified to see his wishes come true. He arrested Magdalene's lover and the other young man and feigned that Ninette was put in a sack and cast

101

into the sea for her crime.

Actually, he took her to her sister Magdalene, with whom he spent the night with the promise that they would meet again in the future. Before leaving, he recommended that Magdalene send her sister away, otherwise he would be forced to prosecute her. Then he went to release the two young men that he had kept in prison during the night.

When they came home, they were surprised to see Ninette alive. They were sure she had been drowned. Magdalene's young lover, suspecting that she had made a deal with the duke, whose passion for her he had perceived, forced her to tell the truth. Magdalene did confess, and the jealous lover killed her with his sword. Then he went to Ninette's chamber and urged her to run away before her presence was noticed. Both ran away eagerly and nothing was heard of them. The next morning, Magdalene's body was found and the other sister and her lover were arrested and held responsible by the duke, who had loved the unlucky victim very much. After suffering painful torture, the two succeeded in bribing their guards and went to Rhodes where they spent the rest of their lives in poverty and distress.

## 34.   A Fatal Attack

William II, king of Sicily, had two children—a son and a daughter. His son died at a rather young age and left a child named Gerbin. The boy grew up handsome and knightly. He was a valiant warrior and a noble soul. His fame reached the court of Tunis; and the king's daughter, a gorgeous lady, fell in love with him without personally knowing him. By the same token, so great was the fame of her beauty that Gerbin fell in love with her from far away. The lady's father was subject to the king of Sicily, and that gave Gerbin a chance to send a secret message to her. She was highly pleased and likewise corresponded to his passion. An underground exchange of messages went on between both young people.

Meanwhile, the princess's father betrothed her to the king of Granada. Since he was a vassal to King William of Sicily, he secured royal authorization to send his daughter by boat to her legal spouse. The princess sent word to Gerbin and told him that she was supposed to reach her promised husband, but expected him to show his bravery. Gerbin, afraid of losing such a beautiful woman, armed two ships and set them along the route she was supposed to follow. As a matter of fact, he intercepted the ship and incited his men to capture it. All the treasures aboard would be given to them, except the princess whom he loved so dearly. They were happy with this deal and moved eagerly for the plunder.

Gerbin ordered his opponents to surrender. The captain of the boat accused him of breaking King William's order. The young man saw the princess on the stern deck and found her far more beautiful than her description. Since her men would not release her to Gerbin, a fight ensued. Then he took a small boat and went to set fire to the enemy's ship. The men aboard, in a desperate move, took the beautiful princess and butchered her before the eyes of her gallant lover. Then they cast her body to him. Like a hungry lion after a herd of cattle, Gerbin jumped on the ship furiously and started to slaughter those people with his hands, teeth, and claws. Then he rescued the body of his beloved from the sea and cried her sad fate. He buried her and went back home, the saddest man alive.

Upon learning of his daughter's death, the grieving king sent a complaint to King William who had authorized the trip. The good king of Sicily could not deny justice. In spite of many entreaties on behalf of his grandson Gerbin, he had him condemned to death and beheaded in his presence. He preferred to be left without an heir rather than be considered a faithless king.

## 35.   Jealous Brothers

Isabel lived in Messina with her three rich brothers. Although she was very beautiful and well-mannered, her brothers had not married her to anyone. Isabel felt attracted to Lawrence, an agreeable young man who attended to her brothers' business. When he perceived her attraction, he dismissed whatever erotic affair he had and developed a genuine love for Isabel. Both lovers found a way to satisfy their passion in secret.

Unfortunately, one night the older brother discovered their romance and, prudent as he was, decided to take counsel with the other brothers. They kept this secret to themselves and dealt with Lawrence in the usual way. One day they took him on a picnic and killed him in a lonely place, where they buried his body in such a way that nobody could discover it. Then they said that Lawrence had been sent abroad on a business trip.

After some time, Isabel started to ask about Lawrence. Tired with her insistence, one of the brothers told her, "What do you have to do with Lawrence? If you don't stop asking, you will receive the right answer."

The poor girl, sad and fearful, spent her days and nights bemoaning the absence of her lover. One night Lawrence appeared in her dream and told her where his body had been buried by her brothers. In the morning, she went for a walk with her trusted maid and found out the truth of her sad dream. Shocked, she cut the head from the rest of the body and brought it home. There she kissed it a thousand times and washed it with her tears. She placed it in a large pot, covered it with top soil, and planted basil on it. She watered the plant with tears and orange-flower water. The basil grew beautifully.

Some neighbors observed Isabel's grief around the pot of basil and notified her brothers of her strange behavior. They had the pot removed in her absence. Again she started to ask for it, and since it was not returned, she wept constantly until she became sick. Intrigued, the brothers turned the pot upside down and saw the human head whose curly hair they suddenly recognized. Afraid to be discovered by the authorities, they buried the head and ran away to Naples. The young lady spent the rest of her life weeping and asking for her pot. She died young, and her sad love story inspired an ancient ballad.

## 36. Foreboding Dreams

Andree was an affectionate young lady from a noble home who had fallen in love with Gabriel, a handsome, pleasant man from a family of lower social standing. They married secretly and would meet in the garden of her house under the protection of a trusted servant. One night she had a very sad dream. She dreamed she was holding her husband in her arms when a dark and frightful thing that she could not discern came out of his body. In spite of her resistance, it dragged Gabriel away from her arms and hid him under ground. She woke up frightened and sent him word not to come to see her. Gabriel insisted on seeing her and, when he heard of her fears, he started to laugh.

"If I believed in dreams," remarked the young man, "I would not be here tonight. For I, too, had a frightening one. I had a beautiful white deer who had become attached to me. In order to keep her with me, I placed a golden collar around her neck and tied a golden chain to it. One day, the white deer was lying with her head leaning on my chest. Suddenly a black dog sprang against me and chewed up my heart. I woke up so frightened that I instinctively touched my heart to see if it was still there."

Gabriel's dream increased the girl's anxiety. They kissed each other several times, but she was always in fear that something dark would come out of the garden. Suddenly Gabriel embraced her with a deep sigh and said, "Ah, my soul, help me, for I die!" And there he fell dead on the ground.

After the terrible shock, the young woman called for her maid and arranged for his burial. It was night still. Both Andree and her maid were carrying the dead man from the garden to the house when a police squad ran into them and took them all to prison. The physicians found no trace of poison in the dead body and thought he died from a sudden burst of an infected tumor close to his heart. The

107

judge in charge of the case, impressed by the lady's beauty, made some amorous advances. Andree rejected him with disdain.

The girl's father was sorry for his daughter's unlucky case. An understanding man, he felt only hurt because she had kept her marriage secret due to the social distance between both lovers. The judge again tried to earn Andree as a wife, but her heart belonged to her dead lover. She and her maid took refuge in a convent and became nuns.

## 37.  The Poisonous Leaf


Simonette was the young daughter of poor parents. Lovely and noble at heart, she fell in love with a young wool worker, who had hired her to spin wool at home. Little by little, a romance kindled between the two. One day he expressed the wish to see her in a garden where they might better enjoy each other's company. She let her father believe she was going to church with her girl friend and instead went to her rendezvous.

He arrived with a friend who took care of Simonette's companion. After the two were alone, her sweetheart took some leaves of sagebush and rubbed his teeth. He said the leaves of that plant were very good to use in cleaning teeth. However, his countenance began to change and he lost his sight and speech. Then he died. His body was swollen and his face full of spots. Simonette burst into tears and called for help. Her girl friend and the other young man ran to her.

"Ah, wicked woman," cried the man. "You poisoned him."

The poor girl was so full of grief that she didn't even think of excusing herself. Other friends of the dead man arrived and dragged her to court. The judge felt that she was innocent, and to make sure he understood the facts, he went to the place of the accident. There Simonette repeated again her story in front of her dead lover and dramatized the past events by taking a leaf from the sagebush and rubbing her gums. While the others were accusing her, the poison worked on her blood and she dropped lifeless on the ground close to her lover's body.

The judge inferred that the sage was poisonous and ordered it cut to its roots. As soon as the gardener leveled the plant, a huge toad appeared, whose venomous breath had infected it. Afraid to approach the beast, the bystanders gathered a large amount of wood lying about and burned it.

# 38. Love and Death

A young Florentine lost his father when still in his teens and was left with his mother, assisted by legal guardians. He grew up with the daughter of a neighboring tailor, and the two youngsters loved each other tenderly. His mother became aware of their mutual passion, but had different plans and tried to break their friendship. She convinced the tutors to pressure the young man into going to Paris where he had his inheritance in a few vested interests. Willy-nilly, the young man was sent to Paris for one year and was induced to stay there another year on different pretexts. Yet, he returned to Florence more inflamed than ever for the tailor's daughter. When he arrived, he found her already married to an honest tent maker.

Afflicted beyond measure, the young man tried to catch the attention of his ex-sweetheart, but she ignored all courting. Unable to repress his passion, he decided to try everything before he gave up. One night, while the lady was out with her husband, the frustrated lover entered their bedroom and hid until they came home and went to bed. When he was sure the husband was asleep, he went to the side of the bed where the lady was lying and put his hand on her breast. She was going to cry out for help when he stopped her and disclosed his name. Trembling, she told him to forget their past love and leave her in peace. If her husband heard him, her happiness would be gone.

The young man evoked, to no avail, their love and mutual promises. Defeated, he asked her to let him lie beside her for a short while, because he was completely frozen due to his long wait. She felt sorry for him and granted this small favor, provided that he would not touch her. Instantly he felt crushed by past memories and his present misfortune and decided to die.

After a while the lady became impatient and started to whisper that it was time for him to go. Afraid that he had fallen asleep, she went to shake him, but was horrified to find him as cold as ice. As soon as she was able to gather her wits, she called her husband and recounted a story of a friend who had gone through the tragic experience that she had just suffered. She asked for counsel for her friend, and her husband said the dead body should be quietly carried to the victim's house and left there. The woman then told him she was victim to the very circumstance and both acted accordingly.

When the dead body was discovered, the physicians agreed he had died of grief. During the funeral, the lady mingled among the other women and went close to the dead body. Suddenly her quenched love came back and she let out a loud shriek. Then she started to cry with warm tears and fell dead upon her ex-lover. Saddened by this tragedy, her husband allowed her to be buried in the same tomb with her unfortunate lover, and so they were reunited by love at death whereas they could not be together in life.

## 39.  The Lover's Heart

Two noblemen, William Roussillon and William Gardetang, had estates in Provence. They were brave, brilliant, and rich. The castles in which they lived were about ten miles apart. The two developed a sincere bond of friendship and loved each other so much that they wore the same colors when taking part in tournaments or other acts of arms. One of them, Roussillon, had a beautiful and lovable wife. The other knight, Gardetang, in spite of his friendship and respect for her husband, fell in love with the lady and found ways to inform her of his passion. Knowing him as a valiant man, she accepted his attentions and in a short time found herself as much in love as he was.

Charmed by their romance, the two lovers behaved less discreetly than they should have, which made the husband aware of what was going on. Roussillon felt hurt, but concealed his intentions better than the two lovers had done with theirs. One day he informed Gardetang that a tournament was being prepared in France and invited him to discuss it. The other gladly accepted the invitation and said he would come to dinner the following evening.

As Gardetang, with two attendants, rode toward his friend's castle to keep his appointment, Roussillon was in ambush with a trusted servant. He rushed out upon his wife's lover and killed him in a rage while the two attendants ran away, not realizing who the murderer was. Roussillon opened his rival's chest with a knife and tore out his heart. When he returned to his castle, he called a cook and told him, "Take this wild boar's heart and make a good dish." To his wife, who was inquiring about Gardetang, he said the appointment had been delayed until the next day.

At dinner, Roussillon was rather inattentive and ate very little. His wife ate the entire cooked heart.

"How did you like it?" he asked, pointing at the empty dish in

112

which the heart was served.

"I liked it very much," she said.

"I believe you," added Roussillon. "It doesn't surprise me that you like, dead, what pleased you most, alive."

"What?" inquired the lady after a doubtful pause. "What did you make me eat?"

"Sir William Gardetang's heart! You, disloyal woman, you certainly did. I took it away from his chest with my own hands a short while ago."

"You have behaved as a disloyal and treacherous knight," she said after a while with her mind full of anguish. "Willingly I gave him my love and I should have been punished for that. Now be it God's will that no other food be mingled with the heart of such a valiant and courteous gentleman!"

She stood up without hesitation and threw herself from a high window. Dismayed, Roussillon saddled his horses and ran away. The bodies of both lovers were buried in the same tomb at Gardetang's castle chapel, and their tragic deaths inspired a few poets.

113

# 40.  The Drugged Lover

In Salerno, the center of the first school of medicine, there lived a famous surgeon far gone in age who married a gentle young lady and kept her well-supplied with jewels and apparel of all kinds. When it came to love, however, he would show on the basis of scientific arguments that it took many days to recuperate. Consequently, the young lady was usually cold in bed because she was poorly covered by her husband.

Since it was sparse at home, there was no other alternative but to apply to somebody else's resources. To this end, she became interested in Roger of Jeroli, a man of noble birth who had lived a lewd and defamed life. He did his best to feed her passion, and the two enjoyed their relations with utmost discretion. The lady would give him good advice and tangible help to reform him of his bad habits and criminal drive.

One day, the old husband had to perform an operation on the decayed leg of a man and prepared an opiate drink to put him to sleep during surgery. The surgery schedule for that evening was postponed because the old man had to hurry to a town where there were many wounded people as a result of mob violence. He left, and his wife called for her lover to spend the night with her.

When he arrived, she locked him in her husband's office until the house staff went to sleep. Roger, alone in the office, started to get thirsty, and since there was no water available, he drank the liquid prepared by the surgeon for his patient. When the young lady came, she found Roger asleep and started to tease him in order to wake him up.

The man, pushed by her, fell to the floor and there he lay unconscious. Frightened, she called her trusted young maid, and both reached the conclusion that he was dead. The lady wept over him, but the maid took a more practical approach. She had seen a pretty large chest displayed before the shop of a cabinetmaker and decided to see if it had been left outside during the night.

She found that the chest was still there and, taking advantage of the darkness, the two ladies carried the body to the place and hid it in that case. The maid wanted to stab him a few times to show it was a crime, but the lady opposed such an idea.

In the meantime, two usurers had plotted to steal the chest. Although they found it rather heavy, they managed to carry it away and set it down in their ladies' bedroom.

At dawn, Roger, having digested the sleeping potion, woke up. He figured that his lady's husband had returned and they quickly had to hide him. He tried to make himself more comfortable, but the chest was not set level on the floor and it fell down with a big bang. The women woke up, but kept silent for fear. Roger, finding the chest open, stepped out and reached a door to get out of the house.

The women, sensing the presence of a stranger, became panicky and started to scream, calling the attention of their men and quite a few neighbors who surrounded the house. Roger, bewildered and amazed, found no way of escape. Since he was known for his past felonies, the police locked him in jail and extorted an easy confession that he had entered the usurers' house to steal. The governor decided to hang him without delay.

The old surgeon came back home and did not find the opiate liquid he had prepared for his patient. He started to ask for it and became angry. The wife, who had other worries on her mind, answered irked, "What's the big fuss over a little jug of water?"

"Water, my eye," replied the surgeon. "It was a sleeping potion."

The lady understood immediately why Roger had looked like a dead body and the news of his intrusion into the moneylenders' house started to make sense to her. The maid, in search of novelties, observed a scuffle between the cabinetmaker and a man who had paid for the chest some time before. The former said that it had been stolen—the latter, that he had resold it.

The two ladies reconstructed what had actually taken place during the night and took counsel to save the unfortunate lover and preserve the lady's honor at the same time. After detailed planning, the young maid went crying to the surgeon and told him that Roger was her lover. She had invited him in during the owner's absence and gave him some water to drink while they were in the surgeon's office. She was very sorry, but she did not know it was medicine. Now she needed his help to save the innocent lover who had been found in the wrong place.

Although angry, the old man was amused by the sad complication and said, "You have given yourself due punishment. You received a sluggard when you thought you had a lusty man who would shake your skin coat. This time I'll help your lover, but it will be the first and last time I do so."

Gratified with this result, the maid went to the jail and coaxed the jailer to let her talk to Roger. After she instructed him on what to say, she gained admission to the magistrate. When he saw her so lively and buxom, he decided to set his grappling hook on that good Christian daughter of God, who did not evade his request. After she was off the grinding job, she told the magistrate how her lover had taken the wrong drink and had been hidden in the chest. The moneylenders had stolen it at night, and now Roger was in trouble.

In the cross-questioning, Roger admitted that he had gone for the surgeon's maid, and the other people involved—the surgeon with his potion, the carpenter with his trunk, the usurers with their theft—confirmed the sequence of facts. The only people to be found guilty were the two moneylenders who received a ten-pound fine.

# THE FIFTH DAY

## Difficult Cases with a Happy Course

## 41.  From Bum to Gentleman

There was on the island of Cyprus a nobleman who was very rich. One of his sons was outstanding in stature and handsome features, but was a hopeless dullard without any aptitude for studies or cultural development. The father, in despair, sent him to his country estates to live among the peasants, something the son liked very much because it befitted his primitive nature. He even adopted the nickname of Cimon, which means brute beast. He lived like a churl and accentuated his rude manners with a rough voice.

One day, he stopped in front of a fountain by which a beautiful lady—Iphigenia by name—was sleeping. Two maids and a man were sleeping close to her. The rough man was enraptured by the extreme beauty of the lady. Her hair looked like gold. Her face was perfect. Her breast, covered with a sheer lace, was delicate. Cimon, growing from an uncouth peasant into a judge of beauty, ardently wished to see her eyes, but repressed his urge to wake her.

After a while, the damsel opened her eyes and saw him standing in front of her. "Cimon," she said, "what are you looking at?" She knew his name because he was a well-known character in town. He gave no answer because he was charmed with both the light and the sweetness of her eyes. The lady felt uncomfortable under his absorbed gaze, called her servants, and told him to go with God. But Cimon offered to accompany her to her house.

Afterwards, he went to see his father, who was displeased at receiving such a visit. Still under the magic spell of his previous encounter, he told his father that he wanted to dress and behave like his brothers. Then he eagerly applied himself to all human studies and, in four years, became a different man. All of this he did with intensity and perseverance in order to gain Iphigenia's love—the first person ever to inspire him with such a noble feeling.

The girl's father rejected Cimon's continuous requests because he had promised her to a gentleman from the island of Rhodes, and had no intention of breaking his word. The day she was sent to her fiancé to arrange the wedding, Cimon, with a group of friends, armed a boat and attacked the Rhodian ship which transported Iphigenia and her group. He cast a big grappling hook to the stern of their ship and, swinging from a strong rope, leaped among them like a lion among sheep. He promised to spare them if they yielded up Iphigenia to him. They accepted, and Cimon took the saddened girl to his boat hoping to console her during the night.

Unluckily, a violent storm changed the boat's course and thrust it into a bay of the island of Rhodes, close to where Iphigenia's original ship had taken refuge. In vain he tried to get out of the bay. The fierce wind made it impossible to sail out. Cimon and his friends were arrested, while Iphigenia was returned to her fiancé. Only his fairness toward the attacked Rhodians saved Cimon from the death penalty. He was condemned to live in prison.

Meanwhile, Iphigenia's wedding was delayed because her future father-in-law wanted to marry, on the same day, another son of his who loved a local girl. The judge who sentenced Cimon was in love with this same girl and was determined to prevent the wedding. He recalled Cimon, whose story he had learned during the proceedings, and decided to get him and his companions as his allies. He called him to his office and told him, in distress, that both Iphigenia and his beloved lady were going to be married by the two brothers. Now he understood Cimon's feelings and proposed a plan to secure both ladies. Cimon felt his spirits uplifted by the new adventure.

The day the double wedding was to be celebrated, Cimon and the young judge jumped into the hall with a group of armed men and stole the two brides, hitting anyone who dared to intervene. Then they escaped in a boat that they had equipped and anchored in a secret spot.

For some time they lived in Crete together with the two ladies who had already become their wives. Later on, thanks to their families' connections they found a way to obtain amnesty and be readmitted to their own countries.

## 42.  Rediscovered Lovers

On a little island called Lipari there was a fair lady named Constance, born of a family of considerable wealth. A young man, Martuccio, fell in love with her, and his affection was returned by the young woman. He was handsome, honest, and industrious. But her family would not consent to the marriage because he was poor.

Determined to become rich, Martuccio gathered together a few friends and convinced them to become pirates under his leadership. Fortune was favorable to their project, and they accrued much money. As often happens, they could not control their drive for more, until one day they were caught by a large fleet of Saracens, their boat was sunk, and those who survived were thrown into jail. The news of this defeat reached the small island of Lipari with the confirmation that Martuccio was killed. Actually he was jailed in Tunis.

Upon hearing the bad news, Constance lost her will to live. She went to the beach and found a small boat with no one in it. She jumped into it, wrapped up her head, and pushed out to sea hoping to find death in its depths. Contrary to her wishes, the boat was pushed by winds to another Tunisian place called Susa. An old Italian lady who lived among Saracens detected the abandoned boat and went to look inside. She found the young lady sleeping and, after awakening her, learned her sad story. She consoled her and convinced her to give up her suicidal intentions. The good woman was poor, but she knew a rich Saracen lady who had a large shop in which she employed many girl workers. The lady felt sorry for Constance and gave her a job and a place to live.

Some time later, a powerful man from Granada declared war against the king of Tunis with claims to his throne. Martuccio, who was in prison, told his guard that he could tell the king a way to win the war. He was admitted before the king and told him that in his previous years he had observed that the Saracens fight their wars mostly with archers.

"That is true," admitted the king.

"You have observed that the archers first cast their supply of arrows and then get hold of those cast by their opponents and keep on fighting. If you deny your enemies any extra supply of arrows after they have cast their own, there is no doubt that they will have to withdraw from the battlefield."

"How can that be done?" inquired the king.

"Secretly replace the conventional ropes on the soldiers' bows with strong but very thin strings. In such a way, they can use arrows with notches that fit only their thin strings. When they run short of arrows they still can use the ones thrown at them; but their enemies cannot use the arrows received from your soldiers because their small notches won't fit the strings in their bows." The king liked this advice very much and won the war in which he was engaged.

After the victory, the name of Martuccio became popular among the Saracens of that kingdom, and Constance, who had learned their language, was delighted to hear the happy news. Her love again grew strong, and she asked her employer to help her reach Martuccio. The Saracen lady, informed of Constance's love, was more than glad to accompany her to Tunis together with the old lady who had first found her ashore. This old woman went to see Martuccio and told him that she had a secret messenger from Lipari who wanted to give him recent news from his hometown.

When Constance saw Martuccio, she ran to him and placed her arms around his neck. He was amazed to see her, for he had heard about her supposed death. They were so happy to be together at last, and the king of Tunis made their reunion happier with lavish gifts and other royal favors.

## 43.  Dangerous Elopement

Angela was the daughter of a modest, but respected family in Rome. Due to her beauty and charm, she inspired the love of Peter Boccamazza, who belonged to an aristocratic Roman family. Their love grew into a genuine tie until each couldn't live without the other. When the young man tried to convince his family to ask for her hand, he found only opposition and obstruction. Determined to make their dream come true, the two lovers decided to elope. They prepared the horses and ran away to a small town which was a few miles away from Rome. There they had friends and relatives who would help them to get married.

On the road, they were occupied in kissing and sporting, so they missed their way and went toward a small castle possessed by Peter's political enemies. It was easy for them to get hold of him, force him to undress, and proceed to plan his execution. Angela succeeded in escaping on her horse.

While Peter was facing his ill fate, a squad of soldiers assailed his torturers, and he was freed. He took his belongings, jumped on his horse, and started in the direction taken by Angela. He rode aimlessly for a few hours, calling her name in all directions, but nothing happened. Night came in the thick wood and he feared that the wolves would eat him. He tied the horse to a big oak tree and climbed up into its branches. The moon rose and he kept awake, cursing his bad luck and weeping for his fair lady. The wolves came and devoured his horse under the eyes of the frightened knight. At daybreak, he saw a fire a few miles away and, as soon as he felt safe, he went there and found a group of shepherds.

Angela had been luckier, or so it seemed. Once she found herself lost, she started to wander without direction and the horse took her to the hut of two old shepherds. They told her it was dangerous for her to live with them because their hut was often attacked by

122

rogues, but they offered hospitality until the next morning. At that time they would take her to a castle nearby.

A short while later a gang of outlaws bumped into the hut. Angela ran and hid in a haystack in the courtyard. The rogues saw the horse and wanted to know who the owner was. The shepherds said the animal was wandering astray by itself. Then the violent outlaws started to search everything and one of them, not knowing what else to do, cast a lance against the haystack which almost hit the hidden damsel. Luckily she held her breath until the gang left with her horse.

The two shepherds were happy to see that she had survived unharmed and, as soon as the morning sun rose, they took her to the castle. The owner was a nobleman who was politically allied with Peter. When his wife heard the girl's sad story, she promised to help her return safely to Rome. As for Peter, everyone believed that he had been killed by his political enemies.

Peter went to join the group of shepherds surrounding the fire, informed them of his misfortune, and moved them to compassion. They led him to a nearby castle, and there he was recognized and welcomed. It was the same castle where Angela had been brought that very morning. There he met his beloved, and the lady of the castle helped them to marry and enjoy their honeymoon in the mountains. Then, they returned to Rome under escort and little by little convinced their families to accept their marriage.

## 44.  The Caged Nightingale

Lizio was a gentleman of good breeding and great worth. In his old age he had a daughter by his wife and named her Cathie. The girl grew up to be charming and fair, and her parents guarded her with care and love. A handsome young man, Richard by name, would frequently come to visit them, and the parents considered him one of their family, unaware that a genuine love was incubating between the two youngsters. One day Richard took courage and expressed his feelings to the girl. "Cathie," said he, "don't let me die for your love."

"Don't you do the same for me," replied the girl. This answer made him more daring, so that he suggested that she sleep that night in the balcony facing the garden. He would manage to reach her, and both would enjoy each other's company. Cathie promised she would try to be there, kissed him hastily, and went her separate way.

It was the end of May, and the girl started to complain to her mother that she had spent sleepless nights because of the excessive heat.

"Heat?" replied the mother. "I don't know what heat you are talking about."

"Mother, you ought to consider that girls feel hotter than ladies in years."

"True," said the mother, "but I have no command over the weather. The coming night may be cooler and you'll sleep better."

"I wish so! But the nights now grow hotter and hotter as we approach summer."

"What do you want me to do?" asked the mother.

"Oh!" replied Cathie. "You and father could let me put my bed on the balcony overlooking the garden. There I would feel better than in our bedroom. I could hear the nightingale sing and might sleep pleasantly."

The mother thought this a reasonable request to console her on-ly daughter and went to speak to her husband. Lizio, who was a rath-er cross-grained old man, wouldn't listen to reason. "Don't come to me with nightingales. I'll have her sleep at the cricket's chirp."

That night Cathie, more for spite than heat, was restless and made it impossible for her mother to sleep. The old lady again ap-proached her husband the next day and brought more pressure to bear on him. As a matter of fact, he gave his assent, provided that a curtain was placed around the balcony. "There she can go to bed and hear the nightingale sing to her heart's content," concluded the old man.

At night, Cathie signaled to Richard when everyone was sleep-ing, and he climbed up to the balcony where she was. They kissed with delight and stayed in bed together making the nightingale sing many times. The nights being short and the pleasure great, before dawn they fell asleep without any cover on because they were over-heated by both the weather and the sport. The girl had her right arm around Richard's neck, holding with her left hand the thing that ladies, for shame, do not dare to name in the presence of men.

The day came, and the old man got up. Curious to know how the daughter had slept, he removed the curtain a little and said to himself, "Let's see how Cathie slept with her nightingale songs." He caught the two young people sleeping in the aforementioned posi-tion. A wise man, he recognized the young lover and went to his wife's bedroom. "Hurry," he said, "come and see Cathie. She caught the nightingale and holds it in her hand."

"How is that possible?" replied the wife, following him. She looked through the curtains and felt like screaming on seeing herself deceived by her daughter right before her husband. But Lizio was a wiser man and convinced her that they should take that opportunity to have the daughter marry such a lusty and noble young fellow. "If he wants to part on good terms," said Lizio, pointing at the sleeping boy, "he'd better put the nightingale in his own cage and not in somebody else's." The wife kept quiet, relieved that her husband was not angry.

Some time later, Richard woke up. "My soul!" he exclaimed. "The day has come. What shall we do?"

"We shall do fine," replied the old man, drawing the curtain. In the ensuing confusion, Cathie hid herself under the covers and

125

Richard begged to be spared his life for his wicked disloyalty. Old Lizio reprimanded him for what he had done, but recognized that youth is hard to control, and all shame and dishonor could be avoided by arranging a quick marriage. Cathie started to cry and beg her father to be merciful and her boyfriend to follow her father's advice. Lizio borrowed a ring from his wife and declared the two husband and wife. "Now take a good rest. You need it," he said and left together with his wife. The two spouses started to kiss each other with a new feeling of happiness after the danger had passed. Since they had not gone more than six miles during the night, before getting up they went two more and put an end to the first day.

After some time they formalized their wedding before their relatives and friends, and nightingaled to their hearts' content.

## 45. Rivals in Love

Two ex-soldiers, both advanced in years, lived in a little town in Northern Italy. One of them died and left a young girl he cared for under the guardianship of the other. She had been found by the late comrade when she was two years old during the siege of Faenza. During the pillage of the defeated town, he had entered a house deserted by the family, except for the little girl. As soon as she heard the soldier enter, she called "Daddy," which moved him to compassion. Now he died happy to see his friend James receive her as a daughter.

James took the girl and moved to Faenza. There she grew beautiful and buxom, and kindled love in two young men named John and Dominic. Both wanted to marry her, but their families were opposed to young weddings. At last, the two young men each tried to obtain her through other means.

The girl's guardian had two servants: one a male, who became friends with John—the other a female, who did the same with Dominic. The two servants promised to let in each young suitor so that he could convince the girl. One night the guardian went to dine with some friends and notice was given to both young men who gathered two separate teenage gangs and went to different spots, awaiting the arranged signal. But the signal was late in coming.

The two servants, unaware of each other's plotting, were together in the same room. Each one was hinting to the other that it was time to go to bed, but neither did. Tired of waiting, the male servant opened the door and made his sign. John broke in and tried to carry the girl away. A noisy struggle ensued, which attracted the attention of Dominic and his gang. The neighbors were aroused, and the whole thing ended in the hands of the police.

The next day, the parents of the two impulsive suitors pleaded for mercy with James, the girl's legal guardian. James said he would be glad to be of help. During the chat, he explained that the girl was from Faenza. One word led to another, and John's father admitted that he had lost a daughter during the town's pillaging and thought that she had been burned with everything else in the house. Anyway, he could recognize his daughter, had she survived, thanks to a scar in the shape of a cross on her left ear.

The girl was brought before them, and the gentleman saw her close resemblance to his wife. He lifted her hair, and discovered the scar on her left ear. Then he started to cry, declaring that he had found his daughter. He began to kiss and embrace her. At first, she opposed the stranger. Then, moved by a mysterious power, she felt the same impulse toward the old gentleman.

The casual discovery was cause of great joy. The city magistrate, affected by such unusual circumstances, was indulgent toward John, the girl's brother who had tried to take her away. Some time later, the other young man married her in a splendid wedding.

## 46.  The Forgiven Seducer

Ischia and Procida are two islands near Naples. There lived two
young people, John and Restituta, both born of two noble families in
those islands, and both ardently in love with each other. One day
Restituta was walking on the seashore collecting shellfish from the
rocks when a group of Sicilians in a boat saw her alone and stole her
away. They took her to Palermo and gave her to King Frederick who
was a great admirer of feminine charms. By chance, at that time the
king was not feeling well. He accepted the beautiful girl and had her
kept under guard in the Cuba, a splendid palace surrounded with
gardens.

When John found out that his beloved girl had been taken
away, he suspected the men in the Sicilian ship, so he equipped a
boat and tried to guess their course. Moving from port to port and inquiring at each stop, he found the place where Restituta had been
locked in. One day he chanced to catch sight of the girl at a window,
and both felt great joy. Since the place was secluded, they arranged
to have a further talk at night.

John studied the building and dared, in the dark, to climb to the
inner side of the garden. There he found a long pole and crept along
it up to his girl's window. In past times Restituta would not let him into her room, coy as she was for her honor's sake, but in the present
circumstance she opened the window and asked to be freed. John
promised that the next night he would bring all means necessary to
carry her away. Carried by love, they enjoyed each other several
times until they fell asleep in each other's arms.

That very night, the king felt better and decided to spend the
night with the beautiful damsel he had been offered a few days before. When he caught the two youngsters naked, embracing in their
sleep, he was suddenly incensed with such a wrath that he almost

129

killed them. But he thought that a base thing for a king to do and decided that the next day they be tied back to back, displayed in public, and burned that evening.

They were tied up, and all the townspeople flocked to observe the two unfortunate naked lovers. As it was to be expected, the men pressed to look at the girl, praising her perfect beauty, while the ladies did the same of John. Moved by such a sensational event, Admiral Roger dell'Oria went to the congested place. First he looked at the girl and commended her fair person. Then he turned to the boy and recognized him without any difficulty. The young couple held their heads down in shame.

"Are you John of Procida?" asked the Admiral.

"My lord, I was," answered the boy, who recognized him. Upon request, he told the man his sad story. At last, he asked for a final grace. "Since I must die," said John, "try to have me turned face to face with her, and I'll die happy."

"Gladly so," answered the admiral laughing. "I'll make sure you may gaze at her till you grow weary of it."

He gave orders not to burn them before the sentence had been confirmed by the king. Then he rushed to the court to meet the king, who held him in great esteem, and convinced him that both youngsters belonged to two noble families whose influence was instrumental in securing the monarchy's power in the islands. King Frederick, after certifying what his admiral told him, regretted his impulsive decision and repaired the injury he had done to both lovers by granting magnificent gifts and sumptuous festivals on their wedding day.

## 47. The Boss's Daughter

A Sicilian gentleman had many children, among them a daughter called Violante. One day a ship of pirates brought a group of boys believed to be Turks and sold them as slaves. Our gentleman bought some of them to use as servants, among them a lad named Theodore. He was an outstanding youngster who had knightly manners and grew to be formal and well-mannered. The owner had him christened and gave him a new name—Peter. So charming was Peter that Violante, the owner's daughter, fell ardently in love with him. It didn't take long for him to notice her feelings because he felt the same.

One day, the ladies in the family went to a country estate for diversion. On the way back, they made the trip on foot. Halfway home, a heavy storm came suddenly upon them. Peter had walked faster with Violante to have a chance to talk to her alone, while the mother, with the other daughters, was left behind. To protect themselves from the rain and hail, they ran into the first house they found.

Peter and Violante found themselves alone in a small hut. To make sure they wouldn't get wet, they had to stay close to each other under a small piece of the roof still intact. From words they soon passed to deeds and, before the storm was over, they had fulfilled their romance completely and made arrangements to carry on their affair in secret.

Everything worked well for a while until Violante found herself pregnant. Peter panicked and decided to run away from his owner, but the girl told him to stay. She assured him that she would never disclose his name. Reassured, Peter remained. But finally she could no longer conceal her pregnancy and revealed her situation to her mother begging her with many tears to save her. The mother insisted on knowing every detail, and Violante stated the events in such a way that she justified Peter's actions.

131

When the time came, the mother took Violante to a country home of hers and assisted her in delivering the child secretly. By a strange coincidence, the father went hunting that same day and decided to stop at the same place. When he caught the daughter crying out, he wanted to know the facts and forced the ladies to say the truth. Enraged, he went back to town and had Peter arrested and tortured. A few days later the unlucky young man was sent to the gallows. On the same day, the father sent a trusted servant with a knife and a poisoned bottle of wine to his daughter, Violante. He gave the servant orders to let her choose her death, either by poison or knife. As to the little boy, he would be thrown to the dogs.

That day, full of sorrow and grief, Peter was led to the gallows. Three noblemen from Armenia, on their way to Rome to arrange a crusade, stopped for some time in that town and heard of Peter's case. They were at the window while the young man, naked to the waist with his hands tied behind his back, was advancing toward the scaffold. One of the three Armenian dignitaries observed that the young man had a red birthmark on his skin and immediately remembered a son of his who would be of the same age. He had been captured by some pirates and sold as a slave.

Instinctively he called out saying, "Hey, Theodore!" The poor prisoner raised his head toward him. "Where are you from and who are your parents?" kept asking the nobleman in Armenian. The young man still remembered his mother tongue and gave the desired answer. The older man thanked heaven for discovering his lost son, went to embrace him, and asked the sergeants to hold the sentence for a while.

The judge informed Violante's father, and the sentence was suspended on condition that the prisoner would marry Violante. Her father found himself in a tragic situation because he now had a chance to marry his daughter to a worthy young man, but he had issued the fatal order to kill her. He immediately sent another messenger who arrived just in time. The first servant was mistreating the girl roughly because she wouldn't make up her mind in choosing her death.

The sudden turn of events found the two young lovers more than willing to abide by the new decision of their parents. The wedding was magnificent, and a few days later Peter took his wife and son to his native country.

## 48.  An Instructive Vision

A noble young man from Ravenna, Nastagio by name, was left very rich after the death of his parents. As so often happens to the young, he fell in love with a lady of his age hoping to inspire her with the same feeling. Although he was a handsome and well-bred man, she not only rejected his propositions, but showed visible dislike for him and his actions. In despair, the unlucky lover tried several times to pay her back the same way, but he was too much in love and couldn't do it. He was spending his fortune trying to impress the cold lady, but all in vain. His relatives advised him to forget her and move elsewhere, but Nastagio went to live with his household in a country residence near town.

One afternoon, he was taking a walk into the pinewood. Suddenly he heard a flurry of noises and crying. He raised his eyes and saw a naked lady followed by two vicious dogs. Behind them, a knight riding a dark horse overtook her. Nastagio had no weapon. He grabbed a pole and ran to help the unfortunate lady.

"Stop!" yelled the knight. "Nastagio, don't meddle in this matter."

"How do you know my name?" asked Nastagio, full of terror and amazement.

"I, too, am from Ravenna, and I knew you before this wicked woman caused me to commit suicide because she was as indifferent and contemptuous as the lady you once loved. After she died, she was sent to hell, too. Now I will follow her one year for each month she abhorred me. Each Friday, I reach her here. I kill her with my pole, and throw her heart to the dogs."

The ensuing scene was frightening. After being slaughtered, the lost soul of the lady recomposed herself and started running again. Nastagio was baffled. He marked the place with a sign and rejoined his friends. The first time they mentioned that he ought to change his way of life, he answered that he would gladly do it under one condition: that they would invite the family of the lady he loved and herself to a banquet to be held the next Friday.

It was not easy to convince the harsh girl, but it was not impossible either. Nastagio set the table at the marked place in such a way that the lady would face the ensuing scene. The dogs, the victim, and the knight appeared promptly. Questioned, the pursuing knight gave the same explanation. The effect of his words was immediate. The same day the girl sent a trusted maid to Nastagio saying she was ready to do whatever he wanted.

"To marry her," replied Nastagio, and the deal went through immediately.

## 49.  An Untimely Banquet

There was in Florence a young nobleman called Frederick Alberighi, highly esteemed for his kindness and deeds of arms. As it
usually happens with most aristocrats, he fell in love with one of the
most beautiful ladies in town, who was married to a rich man. She
was a virtuous woman and ignored his advances. Frederick spent his
fortune in jousts and tournaments to win her love. At last, he was left
with only a small estate in the country and retired there bearing his
poverty with patience.

A few years later, the lady was widowed with a son under her
guardianship. During the summer she vacationed at some property
she owned close to Frederick's. Her son grew familiar with him and
took delight in dogs and hawks. What impressed him most was the
way Frederick's falcon would fly. The boy was so fond of it that he
would have liked to ask for it, but he never dared.

A short time later the youngster fell ill, and the mother, who had
only this son, spent all her time near his bed, eager to satisfy all of his
whims. One day he said, "Mother dear, I feel I would get well soon if
I only could have Frederick's falcon."

The mother knew how much Frederick had loved her without
ever having received a benign look from her. This kept her from
making the request at first, but her love for her son was stronger than
her feminine coyness and she promised she would take care of it.
The next morning, she took another lady along and, by way of diversion, stopped at Frederick's small house. He rejoiced at the great
honor he was receiving for the first time in his life.

"Frederick," said the lady, " I came to make amends for all the
trouble you have suffered for me. Today my friend and I will keep
you company and have dinner with you."

"Madame," answered Frederick with humility, "I do not remember receiving any wrong from you. Let me tell you that I gave to your

135

love whatever I was worth in the past. And for your love I would do everything over again to become poor and receive you as a guest."

That morning for the first time he cursed his bad luck, for he found no money to buy a good dinner for his guests. Finally, he caught sight of his admirable falcon. He killed it and prepared a tasty meal. After they had eaten and talked a while, the good lady felt it was time to tell the true reason of her visit.

"Frederick," she said, "if you had children, you would understand what I am going through. As a mother, I have come on behalf of my son to ask for a gift that you hold very dear. It is your falcon, and if I don't bring it to him, I am afraid he'll become worse."

Frederick heard her words and burst into tears for a long while. The lady thought he loved the bird so much that he couldn't part from it.

"Madame," answered the sad man, "ever since I placed my love in you, I have never had any good luck. But this is the worst of all. I killed the falcon to serve you a meal. I won't ever forgive myself for that."

The lady was depressed at the sad news and blamed him for being so extreme. Yet, she could not help admiring the greatness of his soul. Her son died a few days later. She was still young and rich. A few months later, her brothers pressured her to remarry, and she said the only man she would marry was Frederick Alberighi. Her brothers started to laugh mockingly.

"You may be right," replied the lady, "but I would rather marry a man that needs wealth than wealth that needs a man." And she got her way.

## 50.  A Mismatched Couple

A rich man called Peter Vinciolo married more to deceive people who suspected his homosexual drives than for any real desire of
his own. He took as a wife a hot redhead who would rather have two
husbands than one. Unable to receive any gratification, the lady decided not to waste her youth in forced chastity.

Having thought it over, she became acquainted with one of
those old women who look like a saint feeding snakes, one who goes
for indulgences, counts rosary beads, and talks only about the Holy
Fathers' lives or Saint Francis's wounds. She went to the saintly woman and frankly disclosed her situation. The old woman commended her purpose and assured her that she could arrange an affair
with any man the lady happened to like, provided that she received
some reward for all her prayers and blessings.

One night, the husband went out to have supper with one of his
friends. The wife received, through the quick service of her old woman, a lusty young man. Hardly had they sat at the table to eat when
her husband came back unexpectedly. She did not go to pieces, but
took the young man to a lower room and concealed him under a
hamper, on top of which she cast a sacking. Then she let her husband in.

"Too short that supper of yours," remarked she.

"We didn't even taste it," said the husband.

"How come?"

"I'll tell you. Scarcely were we seated at the table when we
heard someone sneeze. At first we didn't care, but the sneezing kept
on and my friend went to the place and there he discovered his wife's
young lover."

The redhead understood she was not the only sinner in town
and sympathized with the other woman. But she found it easier to
cover her faults by blaming the other woman and started to make all

kinds of fuss. The hypocritical woman! The one everyone believed virtuous and honest!

Her husband was still hungry and asked for his supper. "What?" she yelled with sudden surprise. "Do you think I feel like eating when I am left alone? Am I your friend's wife? Go now, go to bed."

It so happened that a peasant had left his mules without watering them in a stable close to the room where the young lover was hiding. By chance a hand of the hidden man was sticking out of the hamper, and a mule happened to set his hoof on it. The poor man could not help releasing a shriek. The husband ran over to remove the hamper and faced a young man that many a time he had courted for his purposes. This one asked for mercy, and Peter reassured him that he was safe. After confronting his wife, he asked her if they had had supper.

"How could we? You came just in time to spoil it."

"Go then," rejoined Peter, "and set the table. I will take care of the matter to your satisfaction."

They all savored the meal, though both spouses liked it better in bed. At the end, the exhausted stud was not quite sure whether the main entree had come through her front or her husband's rear.

# THE SIXTH DAY

## Witty Answers

## 51.  A Bad Storyteller

Oretta was a witty lady who belonged to the Florentine noble class. One day she was walking with some ladies and gentlemen who had just dined at her house. The way was too long to go on foot. One of the gentlemen invited her to ride his horse and offered to entertain her by telling a story. Oretta accepted gladly and found the plot of the story exciting. On the other hand, the storyteller was a true bore. He would repeat the same word three or even six times and then would correct himself. The lady, tired by such nonsense, told him, "Sir, your horse jolts as he trots. Please help me down." The gentleman took the hint graciously and changed the topic.

## 52.  An Indiscreet Request

Pope Boniface dispatched ambassadors to Florence to discuss some matters with Geri Spina, a very influential leader. Every morning these ambassadors passed before the door of a bakery belonging to Cisti. This baker had the most delicious wines in Florence. He wanted to offer some to the ambassadors, but did not dare take the initiative, so he devised a way to have Geri Spina invite himself to taste the wine.

The day the ambassadors were ready to return to Rome, Geri Spina threw a party on their behalf and invited Cisti. He refused to go to a gathering of aristocrats among whom he would feel out of place. Geri called a servant and told him to go and ask Cisti for some of his wine. The servant, hoping to get some of the wine for himself, took a huge flask and went to Cisti's house.

"Your master didn't send you here," said the baker.

"Where else then?"

"To the Arno River," answered the other.

The servant brought the answer back to Geri Spina who immediately suspected what had gone wrong and told the servant to take a reasonable flask.

## 53. The Unwise Bishop

Bishop Antony d'Orso was an influential prelate in Florence. His niece was one of the most beautiful and pleasant ladies in town. Her husband, although noble, was a very stingy and sordid fellow. A Catalan gentleman, called Diego de la Rata, came to Florence as a representative of his king and fell in love with the bishop's niece. Her miserly husband agreed, against his wife's will, that she spend one night in bed with the gentleman for five hundred gold florins. The astute knight had five hundred silver coins gilded and achieved his purpose. Later on, the trick was discovered, and the husband reaped scorn and loss. But the bishop pretended to know nothing and kept good relations with the Catalan nobleman.

One day both men were riding during a public parade and met Nonna Pulci, a fair and lovable young woman. The bishop pointed her out to the Catalan. Then, he addressed the lady and said, "Nonna, do you think you could conquer this gallant?"

She felt slandered and decided to return blow for blow. "I don't think he would conquer me, for I wouldn't accept fake money."

## 54. The One-legged Stork

Chichibio, the cook of a generous and noble gentleman, roasted a stork for supper. When it was done, its savory smell attracted a young lady from the neighborhood, with whom Chichibio was totally in love. She insisted on getting a thigh of the bird. He tried to deny her request, but at last gave in.

At night, the master brought home a couple of friends to enjoy his meal. When he saw the hen with only one leg, he asked the cook what had happened to the other.

"Sir, storks only have one leg," answered he.

The next day Chichibio, amazed that his lord had not forgotten the incident, had to follow him to a place where there were quite a few storks, all perched on one leg, as they usually do when they rest. Chichibio showed that he was right. The lord yelled, and the storks put their resting legs down.

"Rascal, can't you see now?" said the master in a nasty tone.

"Yes, sir. But you didn't yell last night," answered the scared cook and changed the master's rage into merriment.

## 55.   The Witty Painter

Giotto, the famous Florentine painter, was coming back from his country house with Forese. A sudden storm overtook them, and both men ran to take shelter in a farmer's house.

Since the rain wouldn't stop, they borrowed two cloaks and hats and went on their way. Before they reached Florence, they were completely drenched. Forese looked at Giotto and burst out laughing. "Say, Giotto. If a stranger met us, would he believe you are one of the greatest painters in the world?"

"He would," replied Giotto, "if he looked at you and thought you knew your *ABC's*."

## 56. An Absurd Bet

One day a group of Florentine gentlemen were gathered at a party and started to discuss who were the best and oldest families in Florence. Each one named different powerful families. Michael Scalza mentioned the name of Baroncis (The Cadgers). Everyone at the party started to laugh at him. One of them said he was willing to bet any sum against such an absurd pretension. Michael Scalza accepted the bet, and the host was called to judge the question.

Scalza stated his argument with paradoxical logic. "You know," he said, "that the more ancient a family, the more noble. If I prove that the Cadgers are the oldest family, then they are the noblest. Compare them with the others. Their traits are the most imperfect. Their faces are out of proportions, their noses longer than usual, their chins protruding and turned upward, their jaws like donkeys'. It is obvious that God made them first of all, while He was trying to learn how to draw, just like children do when they first start to scribble. If they were made first, they are the oldest family. If they are the oldest, they are the noblest. And I think I have made my point clear."

The judge and the rest of the party, hearing that comical argument, started to laugh and unanimously agreed that he was right.

## 57. Legalized Adultery

Long ago a cruel law in Prato ruled that any woman caught by her husband committing adultery with a lover should be condemned to death with the same rigor as a prostitute who sells her body. Madame Philippa was in love with a most handsome man and one night was caught by her husband while she and her lover had solace. His first impulse was to kill them. But he contained himself and decided to achieve the same goal through the law.

The lady was dragged before the judge. All her friends and relatives advised her to deny the facts, but she stubbornly decided to challenge the law. Even the judge felt impressed by such a gallant lady. "Madame," he said, "your husband charges you with adultery. According to the law, I should condemn you to death; but I cannot do so, if you do not confess. Look out what you say and tell me if your husband is right to impeach you."

"Sir," replied the lady with poise, "it is true that my husband caught me with this young man that I love with a sincere and perfect love. But you know that the laws are to be just and made with the consent of the concerned citizens. This law discriminates only against women. Moreover, no woman was consulted when it was passed. Now, it is up to you to condemn me. But before you do, please ask my husband if I ever denied him my favors as often as he requested them."

The husband hurried to admit she complied.

"Then," rejoined Philippa, "if he took all he needed, what should I've done with what was left over? Throw it to the dogs? Isn't it better to gratify a lovable gentleman than let it go to waste?"

All the people in the courtroom yelled that the lady was right and moved unanimously that the law be applied only to married women who do it for money.

## 58. Bantered Vanity

Ciesca was a vain and arrogant girl who believed herself to be the most beautiful human being. One day she came back home all full of airs and grimaces and did nothing but huff and puff. Her uncle asked her what was the matter.

"I never saw as many displeasing people as today."

"Dear," replied he, "if you dislike unpleasant people, never look at yourself in a mirror."

The lady, emptier than a reed, understood her uncle's words no better than a ram, although she thought that she was a match for Solomon's wit.

## 59.  The Flouted Mocker

One day the illustrious poet and logician Guido Cavalcanti was taking a stroll. Betto Brunelleschi and a group of his friends spurred their horses toward him intending to mock him. Cavalcanti was known to be an Epicurean, a sect that did not believe the soul to be immortal. People suspected him of being an atheist.

As soon as they reached him, Betto asked him, "Guido, why don't you join us? Why do you waste your time trying to prove that there is no God?"

Guido Cavalcanti was walking along the cemetery. He jumped to the other side of a tomb and said, "Gentlemen, you may tell me whatever you like in your own house."

At first, they thought he was a crackpot. But, then, they understood they had been sharply rebuked, for he indirectly called them dead bodies.

## 60.  The Miracle Peddler

Certaldo was a little town indeed, where Brother Cipolla, a friar of a religious order, used to come once a year to preach his sermon. He was a jolly rascal and a fast talker, and everybody loved to be his friend or well-wisher. One year he announced to the good peasants of Certaldo that he was going to show one of the feathers that fell from the Angel Gabriel's wings during the annunciation of the Blessed Virgin Mary. Two roguish fellows, who knew very well the friar's tricks and appreciated his quick wit, decided to outsmart him. They found out that the friar was visiting a friend far away and decided to take away the announced feather.

Before leaving, Brother Cipolla had reminded his servant to take good care of his belongings. No sooner had he left than his servant spotted a fat maid and ran to her room to engage her in a conversation. The two rogues easily entered the friar's room and found a little coffer with a parrot feather, which they felt sure was the announced thing. They took it away and filled up the coffer with some coals they found in a corner of the room.

The time of the sermon came, and Brother Cipolla began his preaching with a long introduction. The place was full of parishioners eager to see the angel's feather. When the friar felt he had warmed them enough, he recited a prayer with utmost solemnity and had two candles lighted. Then, he unfolded the coffer, pronounced some praises for the Angel Gabriel, and proceeded to exhibit the feather.

As soon as he saw the coals, he did not curse the servant for neglecting his duties, but silently cursed himself for trusting that useless fellow. Yet, he did not betray his feelings. He lifted his eyes and hands to heaven and exclaimed, "God, praised be thy power." Then he addressed the congregation and said that in his youth he had been sent by his abbot to many places throughout the world. And there he started to mention fantastic and distant places which actually

149

were names of streets in Florence.

During his peregrinations, he had collected many sacred relics, such as a finger of the Holy Spirit, a lock of the seraph that appeared to Saint Francis, some rays of the three Wise Men's star, a tooth of the Holy Rood, a vial of Saint Michael's sweat, and so on. He also was able to get some of the coals used to burn the blessed martyr St. Lawrence. By chance he kept those sacred coals in a little casket identical to the one in which he kept the Angel Gabriel's feather. And it was no coincidence that he confused the two boxes.

"God must have inspired me," concluded the witty friar. "For St. Lawrence's feast is the day after tomorrow, and the Lord wants us to remember this saint."

Having thus spoken, he opened the casket and started to chant some versicles in honor of St. Lawrence. Then he showed the coals to the crowd, who looked at them with awe and admiration. The two amused rogues marveled at his quick shift and later on gave him back the feather for further devotional uses.

# THE SEVENTH DAY

## Tricky Wives

## 61. The Unfaithful Sorceress

John Lotteringhi was a Florentine wool comber, luckier in his business than in other things. Being a simpleton, he was often elected president of a religious fraternity and minor officer of other pious groups. He valued those little honors exceedingly and gave generous alms to the members of the clergy in exchange for prayers, hymns, canticles, and like trumpery. His wife was a wise and pleasant woman who got tired of her husband's simplicity and found herself a lusty lover. The two lovers agreed that when a certain sign pointed toward Florence, that meant that the husband would not come home and that the gallant was welcome. He had only to knock three times at the door at due intervals.

One night the husband returned home unexpectedly. His wife had cooked two capons and some eggs to have supper with her lover. Irked by John's arrival, she sent the maid to hide the meal in a convenient place in the garden. Then she had a cold cut with her husband and went to bed.

A short while later her lover came to knock gently at the door. The lady pretended to be asleep in order to avoid any suspicion by her husband.

"Did you hear knocking?" asked the husband.

"Knocking you say? That is a ghost which keeps me frightened."

"Never mind," said he. "I know the *Te Lucis* and other good prayers to dispel the phantom in the name of the Father, the Son, and the Holy Ghost. Amen."

"That sounds good," rejoined the lady, "but I know an exorcism that I learned a few days ago from a holy woman." Both husband and wife agreed to try it and went to the door behind which the lover was waiting impatiently.

"John," said the wife, "you shall spit when I tell you to."

"Fine," replied the husband.

152

The wife started her exorcism. "Phantom, phantom that goes by night, tail up you came and tail up you go. Reach the garden to the foot of the tree, and get an anointed one with hen's turds. Drink from the flask beneath the tree, and don't hurt my John who is with me." Then she turned to her husband and told him, "John, spit."

"Your teeth!" murmured softly the guest outside the door.

The lady repeated her exorcism three times, and her lover, hardly repressing his laughter, went to get the meal and ate it at his ease.

# 62.  The Hidden Lover

A good bricklayer had married Peronella, who worked at home spinning wool. She was a lovable creature, and it did not take long before a handsome young man fell in love with her. She accepted his gallantry and arranged that he would get into her house early in the morning as soon as her husband left to go to work.

One day, the husband came back unexpectedly while Peronella was with her lover. The poor man found the door locked and said to himself, "Blessed be God! He made me poor, but gave me an honest and young wife." He started to knock at the door. The wife recognized his way of knocking and became panicky, suspecting that he saw her lover come in. In a hurry, she hid the young man in a barrel and went to open the door crying her bad luck to have a husband who would stay idle the whole day.

The husband consoled her by saying that he knew what a good wife she was. He had forgotten it was a holiday and there was no work. To make some money, he brought home a man who wanted to buy the barrel for five florins.

"Only five!" exclaimed the wife. "I just sold it for seven florins to a good fellow who is checking to see if it is sound."

The other buyer left, and Peronella told her husband to take care of the deal. The lover, who had missed not even a word, came out of the barrel and faced the husband.

"Where is the lady who sold it to me?"

"I am the husband. You can deal with me."

"Well, it seems all right to me, except some hard dregs which are overcrusted all around. If you want me to take it, you must clean it."

The good husband took a light tool and jumped into the barrel to clean it. Peronella leaned her arms and breasts around the edge of the barrel to see what he was doing and started to tell him to clean here and there as she saw fit. In the meantime, the young lover, unable to carry out his desire the way he normally would, accomplished it as best he could.

## 63.   Sex and Exorcism

Reynold, a nice fellow from a good family, was in love with Agnes, the lovely wife of a neighbor, but never found a way to communicate his desires. She became pregnant, and Reynold tried his best to convince his neighbor to have him as the child's godfather. That afforded him a chance to get closer to the lady, but she never gave in, although she listened pleasantly to his words.

The unsatisfied suitor decided to become a friar. Yet, he never stopped soliciting the lovely mother of his godchild in a subtle and indirect way. The lady slowly started to find him more interesting than in the past and used the argument common to all ladies ready to take that final step: "Do friars do such things?"

"Madam, under this gown I am like any other man."

"Ah!" rejoined the lady. "You are my little son's godfather. How can I do what you ask?"

"Don't be silly," replied the friar. "God forgives all sins. And now tell me. Who is the closer relative to your child: your husband or me?"

"My husband."

"And you go to bed with him, don't you?" asked the friar.

"Of course," admitted the lady.

"Then you can do so more at ease with a stranger like me."

"Goodness, who can answer your wise words!" exclaimed the lady who was not too strong in logic, and let him have a little fun. Using discretion, Reynold went thereafter to see her with a young friar, who entertained the maid with reciprocal delight.

One day, while both religious men were engaged in this kind of celebration, the lady's husband arrived unexpectedly and knocked at the door. The wife dressed quickly and contrived, on the spot, a plan to save the situation. "Dress up and take the child in your arms," she told her lover. "Then listen carefully to my words." She went to open

156

the door partially and addressed her husband. "Dear," she said, "Brother Reynold was sent here by God. Without him, our child would be dead."

"What happened?"

"The child had a sudden fainting spell, and Brother Reynold is reviving him with some exorcism. We couldn't find you to help pray, so we called another friar who is saying prayers upstairs. Now be patient, because only he and the mother can stay in this room."

Brother Reynold had already dressed and asked from inside, "Do I hear your husband at the door?"

"Yes, sir," answered the husband directly.

"Come," replied the friar. "Come and get your child who is safe thanks to our prayers." The father embraced the child with tears. In the meantime, the other friar came down and said, "Brother Reynold, I completed the four prayers you asked for."

"Good for you," replied Reynold. "You have good stamina and breath. I had said only two, but they were enough to heal the child." And there they were, all happy and ready to celebrate the miracle just granted by the Lord.

# 64. The Jealous Cuckold

Tofano, a gentleman married to a fair lady, suddenly grew jealous of her in spite of the fact that she never gave him a reason to suspect her loyalty. Ghita, the wife, could never understand his change of behavior. It occurred to her that he had to be punished with his own disease. Accordingly, she proceeded with discretion and started a fruitful relationship with a handsome man who lived close to her. Having perceived that her husband liked to drink and then fall sound asleep, Ghita encouraged him in this habit. Once he started to snore, she would invite her lover into her house and have fun in safety. So much trust she put in her husband's sleep that she often went to spend part of the night at her lover's house.

The affair went smoothly until one evening the duped husband perceived that Ghita never drank anything while she encouraged him to get intoxicated. Suspecting what was actually the case, the next evening he pretended to be drunk when he came home. So well did he play his part that Ghita believed it and went to her lover's house. No sooner had she left than he sprang out of bed and locked the door from within. Then he leaned out of the window waiting for her to return.

A few hours later, the lady came back, found herself locked out, and tried to open the door.

"Forget it," yelled the husband from the window. "You'd better go back to where you have been." The night was completely dark. There were no lights in the streets of ancient towns. The wife begged, entreated, wept, but to no avail. Then she threatened him.

"What can you do to me?" asked Tofano scornfully.

"I'll shame you," said she. "I'll throw myself into that well, and people will hold you guilty of murder."

The silly husband was not moved by her words. She took a big rock, went to the well, and dropped it in, yelling in distress, "God pardon me."

Scared, Tofano grabbed a rope and a pail, hoping to save her. As soon as he went out, she entered the house and locked herself in. The fooled husband begged, threatenend, then lost his patience and started to yell aloud, upsetting the entire neighborhood. He began to explain, but the harder he tried to sell his side of the story, the easier it was for people to buy his wife's version of the facts.

## 65.  Jealousy and Adultery

A rich and respected merchant from Rimini was in love with his wife. She was beautiful and charming and did her best to please him. She had a wonderful personality and everybody was pleased with her. Suddenly, this aroused a violent wave of irrational jealousy in her husband who curtailed all her activities and social contacts. He went so far that the poor wife couldn't even look out of the window. Her life was wretched, and she decided to treat him in such a way that he would repent.

She knew that an agreeable young man lived in the house next to her. She and her maid explored the whole house and discovered a crevice in the wall which opened into the young man's bedroom. She called him softly and started to brief him on her sad condition. The young man sympathized with her, and both of them enlarged the crevice to such an extent that they could touch hands.

On Christmas Eve, the lady told her jealous husband that she wanted to confess. Such was his jealousy that he contrived a base plan in agreement with his parish's pastor, who assigned a new priest for her confession. The wise lady immediately recognized her husband under the disguise of his priestly garb and confessed that she had an affair with a priest. The jealous man felt a knife piercing his heart, but stood fast.

"Doesn't your husband stay in bed with you?" asked he.

"He does."

"How can the priest lie with you, too?" he wondered aloud.

"I don't know exactly. But he pronounces certain mysterious words and finds all doors open. My husband falls asleep, and the other never fails to come."

"You should prevent him from coming," retorted the confessor.

"Oh, no!" said she. "I love him, too."

"Too bad," replied the disguised husband. "I cannot give you absolution."

"I am sorry. I didn't come here to tell you lies," concluded the lady.

Caught in his guise, the husband had to give in, but arranged to say special prayers for her and promised he would send a young clerk daily to find out how things were proceeding. The lady begged him not to send anyone to her house because her husband was very jealous, but the pseudopriest insisted, and the arrangement was agreed upon.

On her way home, the lady sensed from her husband's behavior that she had given him a bad Christmas. At night, he told her that he had an engagement with some friends and went outside to hide himself close to the entrance with weapons. The wife locked all the doors and informed her young lover, who came to her through a window on the roof. While the jealous husband kept close watch on the street door, the two lovers had a good time until daybreak.

He came back in the morning shivering with cold and slept during the day. Then he sent a young clerk to the wife to find out if a certain person had shown up. She sent word that no such a visit had taken place. Happy that his night watch had been effective, from then on the fooled husband kept spending the nights out with the same purpose while the two lovers renewed their happy meetings.

At last, the jealous man couldn't hold his secret any longer and told her, "Disloyal woman, you love a priest. Tell me his name."

The lady began to smile and said, "Don't you think I knew who was the priest who confessed me on Christmas day? I told you I loved a priest. Weren't you yourself a priest at that moment? I told you I go to bed with a priest. Can you deny that I do? Can you deny that such a priest finds all doors open in the house?"

The poor man admitted his poor behavior and put his trust in his wife. She made good use of it, for she could not bear the sight of her lover crawling on the roof like a cat, and let him in discreetly through the main door.

## 66. The Unexpected Husband

A young woman, Isabel by name, was married to a valiant and rich gentleman. She got tired of him and fell in love with a well-bred young man who reciprocated her passion. In the meantime, another man, Lambertuccio, fell in love with her and tried everything to entice her. Finally, he lost his patience and sent her a message that he would dishonor her if she did not submit to his will. The frightened woman, knowing his temper, said that she would comply at the proper moment.

One day when she was alone, she sent for her young lover. While they were sporting in the bedroom, the maid brought news that Lambertuccio was coming. Isabel hid her lover behind the curtain, graciously received the temperamental suitor, and asked him what had brought him to her house. He started to kiss her and said that he had seen her husband leave. He locked the bedroom door and started to take his pleasure.

Again the maid knocked at the door, saying that the lady's husband had arrived unexpectedly. Isabel felt like dying. Immediately, she got up and told Lambertuccio to leave yelling angrily, "I'll find him somewhere. I'll find him." He did as she said.

"What's the matter with that crazy fellow?" asked the husband as he came up the stairs.

"What a scare!" replied the wife, putting up a show. "A poor young man came running in and asked me to hide him from that man, Lambertuccio. I felt sorry and let him in. Lambertuccio saw my opposition and left moaning and threatening."

"Well done," said the husband. "I am glad you kept any trouble away from our house." Then he added, "Where is the other man?"

"I don't know where he is hiding."

The young lover who had caught on the lady's plan came out trembling and explained that Lambertuccio must have mistaken him for someone else. The husband felt sorry for him and took him home under his protection.

## 67.  The Esquire's Passion

Ludovico, the son of a rich Florentine, heard some noblemen talk of the famous ladies of their times, and all agreed that Madame Beatrice from Bologna was charming above any other woman. Enticed by her fame, he decided to go to her town and meet her. When he saw Beatrice, he felt an ardent love and took a job among the servants of her husband in order to be close to her.

One day the husband went out of town, and the lady, who was not aware of the servant's love, decided to play chess with him. He adroitly contrived to let her win. When all the ladies were gone, he heaved a sad, deep sigh. The lady asked what the cause of this was, and he heaved an even heavier sigh. She became intrigued and pressured the young man to talk. In a discreet way, he explained the circumstances that brought him to her service and asked her to let him serve her secretly for the rest of his life, if possible. So touched was she by his love that she promised to do for him what she never thought of doing for any man. She would satisfy him if he went to her side of the bedroom at midnight.

He went in punctually and found her awake. She took his hand in the dark and held it tight. Then she awoke her husband and asked him who was his most trusted servant. Bothered, he answered that it was Ludovico.

"You'd be surprised," said the woman. "He asked me to surrender to him. If you want to catch him red-handed, disguise yourself with my dress and go to the meeting place."

The husband went out and Ludovico, who had tried to escape her grip cursing her and her love, came in. After a good, a very good while, she sent him to the garden with a stick, pretending that he had

164

put her virtue to a test. He went and attacked the husband dressed in womanly attire. "You bad woman!" he yelled, "I'll tell your husband tomorrow morning."

The husband ran home under a shower of blows and so impressed was he with his trusted servant that from then on Ludovico's love for Beatrice went smoothly.

# 68.   A Crafty Wife

Harry Berlinghieri, a prosperous Florentine businessman, decided to marry an aristocratic woman, who did not make a good match for him. As a matter of fact, she fell in love with an ex-suitor of hers and found a way of engaging in a love affair in spite of her husband's careful surveillance. She had discovered that Harry would stay awake until late to make sure she was sleeping. Then he would sleep soundly as a log. To achieve her purpose, she would tie a string to her toe and cast it out of the window so that her lover could pull it from outside. If she released the string, it meant that her husband was sleeping and she would open the door for both to spend a few hours together.

This artifice went on for some time. One night the lady fell asleep, and the husband stretched out his leg. He felt the string and discovered the whole arrangement. Suspecting what was going on, he gently cut the string from the wife's toe and tied it onto his. After a short while, the young lover came and pulled the string as usual. The husband had not fastened it well, and it fell down. He went to open the door, but he did so in a way that made the lover suspicious. Eager to know the truth, the husband went after the intruder, and both men began to run in the dark.

Meanwhile, the lady woke up and saw the cut end of the string on her toe. She understood what had happened and felt alarmed. Immediately, she called her trusted maid and begged her assistance. She told the maid to take her place in bed and receive her husband's blows. She would give her a well-deserved reward. Then she hid herself in another room, waiting for the storm to come.

And it was not long in coming. Harry, frustrated because he was not able to recognize his wife's lover, discharged his rage against the unfaithful lady. Finally, he cut her hair, saying he would go and call her brothers to dishonor her. When they heard the story, they decided to punish her, although their mother was recommending moderation towards their sister. The brothers went in enraged, but found her attired like a lady who had not yet gone to bed. She was sewing by candlelight and showed none of the marks her husband had described. Harry looked at her as if he had lost his wits.

The lady took full advantage of the new situation and made herself the victim of a drinker who never came home on time. She said he would go around the taverns and fool with lewd women, and probably had had that strange adventure with some other woman. In any case, she asked her brothers to be considerate towards him, in spite of the fact that her mother, who had first recommended peace and moderation, now insisted on punishing a vulgar merchant who thought he could buy everything and everyone with his money.

## 69. The Overcautious Lover

Nicostratus had married a spirited and beautiful young woman called Lydia. He was wealthy and would supply his wife with all she wanted, except one thing. He was approaching old age and only enjoyed hunting with dogs and hawks. Deciding to get her share of fun, Lydia fell for Pyrrhus, a young servant who was trusted and loved by old Nicostratus.

She could not resist her passion any longer and opened her heart to Pyrrhus through her maid. Taken by surprise, the young man answered that he could not believe his ears. No matter how much he admired Lydia, she was far above his social status. Moreover, he thought that her proposal was a trap set by both husband and Lydia to test his loyalty. When the maid heard his reasons, she called him a jerk.

Lydia felt like fainting from frustration. A few days later, she sent back her maid with the same message. The maid stressed how much the lady was suffering and told him to set aside all his scruples. The young man had thought the proposition over and had reached other conclusions. He said that he wanted some proof that she was not setting a trap for him.

"What proof?" said the maid.

"I ask for three things. Lydia has to kill her husband's favorite hawk. She has to pull a lock from her husband's beard. Finally, she has to send me one of her husband's teeth." These were hard conditions, but Lydia went ahead with them.

One day when her husband had some friends at home, she grabbed his best hawk and cast him against the wall. The innocent bird died, and she explained her act by saying that because of that hawk her husband would neglect her to go hunting.

The second condition was fulfilled one evening when Lydia was frolicking with her husband. He pulled her jokingly by the hair. She

168

replied by pulling out a little lock of his beard, and immediately she sent it to Pyrrhus.

Finally, Lydia tried to satisfy the third condition. She convinced Nicostratus that he had bad breath because of a rotten tooth. With her maid's help, she pulled it and the benighted husband said that he felt better already. Lydia was glad she had carried out her difficult task.

Now she wanted to satisfy her pleasure in a rather curious way and had Pyrrhus instructed by her maid. Pretending to be sick, she was carried by her husband and the young lover under a pear tree. After a while, she craved some pears. Pyrrhus climbed up the tree, but immediately felt scandalized and started to reproach the old man. "Sir," he yelled, "how do you dare do such things under my eyes? Do you think I am blind? Don't you have enough room in your palace!"

"What's the matter with him?" asked Lydia. "Does he rave?"

Nicostratus became curious and was surprised to find out that, from the tree, Pyrrhus had seen him make love to his wife.

The two spouses were astonished and agreed that such a marvel must depend on some mysterious virtue of the tree. Eager to satisfy his curiosity, Nicostratus started to climb the tree. When he turned his eyes downward, he, too, saw his wife and Pyrrhus having sex together. Upset, he started to insult the two lovers. Then he came down cautiously and found both of them as quiet as they were before his climbing. The wife, upset that her husband had questioned her morality, had the tree cut and found better ways of carrying out her business.

## 70. Forgiven Adultery

Two young men from Siena were close friends. One was called Tingoccio—the other, Meuccio. They were such good friends that they promised each other that the first to die would come back and report to the second about the other world.

After making this agreement, Tingoccio was invited to be the godfather of a child just born to Mita, the young wife of his friend Anselm. This gave him a chance to become familiar with Mita, who was a beautiful woman. Both Tingoccio and Meuccio fell in love with her, but neither one dared confess it to the other. Tingoccio was afraid to be censured because he seemed to abuse his condition as a godfather. Meuccio perceived that his good friend had a lead over him and didn't dare make him jealous. Actually, the former had a better chance to show his feelings to the lady and achieve his goal. But he exerted so much effort in his amorous labors that he became sick and some time after died. The third day after his death, he appeared to Meuccio at night time.

"Who are you?" asked Meuccio upon seeing the ghost in his room.

"I am Tingoccio. As you see, I keep my word."

The two talked a lot about the other world. Before Tingoccio's soul took leave, Meuccio remembered his friend's love affair and asked if there was a harsher penance for people seducing a godchild's mother.

"Not at all," replied the ghost. "When I arrived down there, I was frightened I would deserve a heavier sentence and started to shiver in fear. But an older soul mocked me and told me to forget about my past."

Meuccio was glad to hear this and, from then on, he felt no inhibitions whenever he bumped into some desirable godmother.

170

# THE EIGHTH DAY

Hoaxes and Conjugal Triangles

# 71. A Wife's Loan

Gulfard was a German officer in the payroll of the state in Milan. A stout and loyal fellow, his credit rating was excellent, for he repaid each loan he received. During his stay in the city, he fell in love with the wife of a rich merchant and in a discreet way let her know his feelings. The lady sent him word that she would please him, provided that he satisfy her need of two hundred florins and keep their affair an absolute secret.

Gulfard despised her sordid covetousness, but let her know that he would do everything in his power to please her. Nobody would know anything except a trusted friend of his, who always kept him company.

One day the lady informed Gulfard that her husband was to leave town in a day or two. Gulfard went to him before he left and took a loan for two hundred florins. The rich merchant left town, and the German officer, taking his friend along, went to deliver the two hundred florins to the lady. "Madame," he told her in his friend's presence, "take this money and give it to your husband on his return."

"Gladly," answered the lady, thinking that he had said this to cover up his real purpose before the friend. She counted the money and was happy. Then she obliged Gulfard every night until her husband returned.

Later, when Gulfard spied the merchant with his wife, he went with his friend to their house. At the proper moment he said before everybody, "Sir, I had no use for the two hundred florins you loaned me. Therefore, I returned them to your wife during your absence. Please cancel my debt."

The merchant asked his wife if she had received the money, and she could not deny it in front of the other witness. Therefore, she gave her husband the price of her baseness, and Gulfard had the last laugh in this sordid affair.

172

## 72. The Sexual Urge of a Priest

The pastor of Varlungo, a little village near Florence, was a lusty man who always tried to please the ladies in his parish. Among them, Belcolore, the wife of a farmer, was most to his liking. A jolly young woman, she was as apt at turning the mill as any woman alive. She could play tabor, lead the dance around, and sing. He tried all means to attract her attention, but she ignored him, even though he kept sending gifts from his garden.

One day, the priest saw Belcolore's husband leave the village on some business. Immediately, he ran to see her and started to complain about her harshness.

"What am I doing?" she asked with a mocking laugh.

"You don't do anything. Nor do you let me do anything. That's what is wrong," answered the pastor.

"Come on, now. Do priests do such things?"

"Better than others," replied he. "And I'll tell you why. We grind seasonal, not steady harvests."

"What do I care?" asked Belcolore. "All priests are stingier than the devil."

"What do you wish? A pair of shoes? A headlace? A waistband?"

"I need five florins by next Saturday."

"It's too bad I don't have them handy, but I'll get them before next Saturday," promised the priest.

"You are all the same—generous in promises, and afterwards there is nothing to it. Remember what you did with Biliuzza? You won't play the same trick on me."

The priest convinced her to accept his cloak as a deposit, and both got into the barn to have a good time. But when he went back home without his cloak, he felt bad at the thought of wasting five florins on one episode. Being shrewd, he sent a young clerk to the

173

lady. He asked her to lend him a mortar, pretending that he had to prepare some kind of sauce for two of his friends.

Later on at dinner time, the priest saw the woman eating with her husband. Again he sent his young clerk to the woman with her mortar. "Madam, the reverend thanks you very much. Here is your mortar. Please give back the cloak he left as a token."

The woman was going to say something, but her husband stopped eating with an abrupt gesture. "What?" he said. "You took a pledge from the reverend? I should break your neck. Give it back and, in the future, lend him anything he wants."

Grumblingly, she returned the cloak. "Tell His Reverence that he will never pound sauce in my mortar."

The clerk brought the message to the pastor. "When you see her," replied the priest, "tell her we'll be even. If she doesn't lend me her *mortar*, I won't let her have my *pestle*."

## 73.  The Magic Stone

Calandrino, a simple-witted painter, overheard a talk between
two fellows who had arranged a practical joke at his expense. One of
them described the virtues of different stones as authoritatively as if
he were a famous lapidary. Calandrino asked where the stones could
be found. They mentioned a fantastic place in a country called Ben-
godi, where the vines are tied up with sausages and there is a moun-
tain of grated Parmesan cheese which people throw on top of huge
meals of raviolis and macaronis. Amazed, Calandrino asked if any of
the marvelous stones were to be found close to Florence. "Yes,"
replied the big jester. "There are two kinds. The first, when ground in
the mill, becomes flour. The other kind, heliotrope, is a black stone
of great virtue. Whoever finds it becomes invisible and cannot be
seen by any person around."
   "Where can it be found?"
   "A few miles away from here, in the Mugnone River."
   Calandrino noted all the man's remarks and ran excitedly to his
friends, Bruno and Buffalamaco—two merry fellows, very shrewd
and well-advised. He wanted them to stop painting and follow him to
look for the heliotrope. "Think of it," said Calandrino. "We can go
around the money changers' desks without being seen and get rich
fast." The two friends winked at each other and told him to wait until
next Sunday when they could go without attracting the attention of
other people.
   The three left early in the morning. Calandrino was so eager
that he moved ahead of his two friends, and once in the Mugnone,
started to grab all the black stones he could find and fill up his pockets
and chest. Later, Bruno and Buffalmaco saw that noon was near and
put this plan into action. Pretending not to see their foolish friend,
Buffalmaco asked, "Where is Calandrino?"

175

"I don't know. He was here just a minute ago," answered Bruno.

"I'll bet you he went home and played a joke on us."

"We were fools to believe in the virtue of those stones."

Calandrino heard them with great delight and concluded that the heliotrope had fallen into his hands. He said nothing and was determined to go back home. His two friends threw rocks all around to unload their frustration, hitting the poor simpleton many times. He bore all that in peace and went back home. Since it was noon, people were eating and almost nobody was on the street to pay attention to him. The poor fellow became more and more convinced that he had gotten hold of the mysterious stone.

He reached home with his heavy load of stones and found his wife, a fair and virtuous lady, at the staircase. Seeing him in his condition, she began to rail him. But Calandrino, chagrined at being seen, exploded furiously, "Wicked woman, you have ruined me!" He dropped his stones and started to kick and hit her.

Meanwhile, the two friends arrived at his house and prevented him from mistreating the innocent woman with the excuse that God wanted to punish him for his intention of cheating them after he had found the heliotrope.

## 74. The Trapped Priest

Madame Piccarda was a young widow of noble birth. She was not very rich, but lived comfortably in a nice house with her two brothers. She used to go to the cathedral, and the rector—a seasoned priest—fell helplessly in love with her. He was a witty man, but full of arrogance and conceit. His love propositions got nowhere, but he never lost a chance to solicit her favors.

Annoyed, she pretended that she could not resist his courting any longer and declared herself ready to surrender. The old fool was amazed that she could resist so long and arranged a meeting in her house. Since she lived with her brothers, there was only one way to avoid a scandal. He would enter her bedroom stealthily and stay in absolute silence in her company. The priest agreed.

Madame Piccarda secured the help of her ugliest maid. Her nose was flat; her mouth, twisted; her teeth, big and ill-set; her complexion, green and yellowish. At night, the priest went to the bedroom and silently enjoyed the woman he found in bed.

In the meantime, the lady's brothers went to invite the bishop to have a drink in their house, and he accepted. After a while, they suggested that he see something surprising and led him into the bedroom, where the naked priest was sleeping with the ugly maid in his arms. The bishop ordered a forty-day punishment for the foolish rector. Shame and frustration afflicted him much longer.

## 75.   The Fooled Judge

A judge, sordid in his life and despicable in appearance, was hired by the mayor of Florence. Three citizens were surprised to see such an outlandish character, with his dirty bonnet and greasy gown, hold an official position. When he sat on the bench, a pair of breeches came halfway down his legs. The three decided to mock such a ridiculous magistrate. One of them, without being seen, crept under the bench and posted himself at the judge's feet. The other two fellows went to each side of the judge and started to plead a supposed altercation.

"Your Honor, tell that thief to return my gaiters to me," one would yell and drag the judge to his side.

"Your Honor shouldn't believe him! He accuses me in order to hide his guilt. He stole my bag and now comes with a different story," yelled the other and pulled on the opposite side.

Each one kept yelling and pulling at the same time, and the confused judge swiveled from side to side, trying to understand what was going on. The third fellow, who was under the bench, grabbed his breeches and took them down suddenly. The judge felt the jerk, but did not realize what it meant. Therefore, he pulled his clothes up and tried to fix his breeches, but failed to find them. Meanwhile, the two noisy plaintiffs went out and the one under the platform joined them. The judge swore to avenge such an insult made to a member of the bench, but the mayor realized that he'd better appoint more decent judges for his jolly citizens.

# 76.  Robbed and Fooled

Calandrino owned a small farm, not too far from Florence, which was a part of his wife's dowry. Among other things, he fattened a pig every year and killed it to salt its meat.

One year, his two friends, Bruno and Buffalmaco, heard that his wife was not going to the farm and decided to fool her simpleminded husband. They went to see Calandrino, who proudly showed what a fine pig he had killed. The two friends told him to sell it and have a ball with them in the tavern, but he resisted any temptation because he was afraid of his wife.

"Don't be silly!" both friends told him. "Make her believe that the pig was stolen." No matter how much they insisted, it was impossible to convince him. So they decided to trick him.

At night, the two men invited Calandrino to the tavern, and the good priest who was with them offered to pay for the drinks. Taking advantage of such generosity, Calandrino drank as much as he could and before long he was intoxicated. They took him back, put him in bed, and stole the pig.

The next morning, Calandrino woke up after having slept away the fumes of the wine. He became aware that the pig had been stolen and started to cry like a child. Bruno and Buffalmaco came to see him and he greeted them with the sad news.

"My pig has been stolen."

"I am glad you finally did it!" answered Bruno.

"I'm telling you the truth," Calandrino said, still crying.

"Cry louder," replied Bruno. "People will believe you more."

"Good, good," went on Bruno. "Make yourself heard, and then it will seem true."

"You drive me crazy," exploded Calandrino.

"Come on," said Bruno. "I saw it only yesterday. It couldn't have flown away."

179

"That's the way it happened," confirmed the other, weeping. "My wife will never believe me."

Convinced that he said the truth, both friends changed tone and offered to help him. He should throw a party for his neighbors and treat them with ginger boluses. Every innocent person could eat them easily. But, if the thief were to take one, it would taste as bitter as poison. To carry out their plan, Bruno and Buffalmaco asked a friendly druggist to prepare two dog balls with fresh syrup of hepatic aloes and coat them with sugar.

At night, all the neighbors came to the party willing to face the test. They drank, chatted, and socialized. Then Bruno passed the boluses around. When he came to Calandrino, he gave him the marked one. He started to chew it, but spat it out immediately. Everyone became suspicious. Bruno came back and gave him the other ball. Calandrino took it eagerly. If the first seemed bitter, the second one was much worse. Ashamed to spit it out, he kept it in his mouth while tears were running copiously down his face. Finally, he couldn't help spitting the whole thing out. That did it!

After the guests were all gone, Bruno and Buffalmaco decided to blackmail him and requested two capons each if he did not want his wife to be informed of his tricks.

## 77.  The Scholar's Revenge

Helen, a young Florentine lady, belonged to a rich and re-
nowned family. She was left a widow and chose never to marry
again. She preferred to enjoy life with a handsome youth she loved.
It happened that Rinieri, a young scholar, returned from Paris where
he had dedicated himself to the pursuit of knowledge and truth. He
saw Helen and fell in love with her. His courting became persistent.

Eager to play a practical joke on him, Helen invited him to her
courtyard at night. The maid locked the door and told him the lady
would see him as soon as she could. Helen spent the evening dining
with her lover and then started to tease him for being jealous of the
scholar. Both of them were in the mood to ridicule Rinieri who was
waiting in the snow-covered courtyard.

Twice they sent the maid to tell him that the lady was sorry for
being late. A brother of hers had come unexpectedly and was keep-
ing her company. Then both went to bed and spent a long while in
merriment and solace while the unlucky scholar was dancing on the
ice to the sound of his chattering teeth. To get more fun, Helen went
down to the courtyard door and called to Rinieri in a low voice
through a little hole. The poor man thanked God for his imminent
rescue and ran up to the door.

"Please let me stay inside and I'll wait for you."

"How can I?" she said with false tenderness. "This door is noisy
and he would hear us."

"Then go soon and prepare a good fire. I'll need it badly when I
come in," replied the scholar. She went in with her lover, and they
slept very little because both had a good time laughing at Rinieri. He
waited in vain and finally understood that he had been fooled by the
lady.

At dawn, the maid came to open the door and let him out. She apologized for the unfortunate incident. Rinieri acted wisely and repressed all of his hate. "In truth, I have had a very bad night," he admitted. "I know your lady is not to blame. She came down to show her compassion. What wasn't possible tonight will happen some other time." He went home to take some rest, but was crippled by the cold. In time he recovered and prepared to take full revenge. But he always pretended to be in love with the young widow.

After a certain time, Helen was abandoned by her lover and pined for him tearfully. The maid, anxious to help, suggested to her that the scholar might lend a hand with some black magic he had learned in Paris. The mistress, in her dejection, did not realize that Rinieri would use such magic for himself if he knew it. She was so eager to get her lover back that she sent her maid to arrange a deal with the scholar and promised to be generous with him if he helped her out.

A few days later, he met with the lady to work out the details. He said that only a brave woman could go through the magic ritual. He had to make a statuette of her lost lover and, once it was ready, she should plunge naked seven times into a river in the moonlight. There she should go naked to the top of a solitary building and repeat seven times certain words he would teach her. Two damsels would appear to carry out her wishes, and then she could dress up again.

"That suits me," replied the lady. "I have an estate close to the river with an uninhabited tower nearby. It is July, and I don't mind bathing at night." Again Rinieri reminded her of her promise to satisfy his love, and she said she would.

The night came when Helen put the plan into action. She went alone to the river, hid her clothes under a tree, took her seven baths, and went to the top of the tower to perform the ritual. Rinieri hardly could hold his breathing and control his passion when the naked lady passed close to the bush where he was hiding.

As soon as she was on top of the tower, he quietly went to remove the ladder. Helen finished her prayers and waited for the two angelic damsels. After a long while, she realized that she had fallen into the scholar's trap and fainted. When she came to herself, she started to weep and plead.

Rinieri reminded her what he had suffered on a snowy night in her courtyard while she was having fun with her ungrateful lover. In one single night, he had learned more than during years spent studying in Paris. He left her alone, went to dine with a friend, and had a good night of sleep. The next day, he informed Helen's maid of her whereabouts, and she rescued the exhausted, sun-burned, but wiser lady who had learned the hard way that it does not pay to make a fool of a man, especially if he is a learned scholar.

## 78. Unplanned Wife Swapping

Two young men, Spinelloccio and Zeppa, were next-door neighbors and very close friends. Both of them were married, and their wives were fair and pleasant women. It happened that one of them, Spinelloccio, developed a close familiarity with the other friend's wife, and finally succeeded in going to bed with her. The affair went on unnoticed until one day Zeppa remained at home without his wife's knowing it. He saw both lovers in bed and felt sorely angered. While the two were having a good time, he planned how to avenge his hurt pride.

As soon as the friend left, Zeppa went into the bedroom. The wife, caught by surprise, could not deny what had happened and promised to cooperate with her husband in order to get his pardon. He told her to arrange another appointment with her lover for the next day, which she did. During the morning, Zeppa had a business meeting with his wife's suitor. At the fixed time, the latter left the meeting with the excuse that he had arranged to lunch with some friends. Thus he went to his amorous engagement.

While the two lovers were carrying out their business as usual, Zeppa came back home. His wife made a show of fear and locked her lover in a chest. Then she went to prepare a meal for her husband. Zeppa told her aloud, "Listen, Spinelloccio went to lunch with some of his friends. Why don't you invite his wife to eat with us?"

She went to call her, and the lady accepted the invitation. But instead of being entertained in the dining area, she was locked in the bedroom with Zeppa. She was puzzled when he started to kiss and pet her. She tried to resist, but he told her what had happened between her husband and his own wife and convinced her easily of the whole truth. To make his proposition more acceptable, he promised to give her a precious gift at the end. Then he embraced her, laid her on the chest where her husband was hidden, and gave free course to his appetite.

Spinelloccio heard everything from his hideout and felt like dying at what was going on over his head. But soon he realized that the messy situation he had started justified Zeppa's behavior. After the lively folk dance was brought to its conclusion, the lady asked for the promised jewel. Zeppa called his wife who came with a smile, happy that all of them were on equal terms.

"Open the chest," Zeppa said to his wife. She did, and the promised jewel came out. Both men, laughing at the past, decided to forget their mistakes and keep their friendship alive. Actually, they became better friends than ever and decided to share everything, including their own wives.

# 79. The Silly Physician

Master Simon had graduated in medicine from the University of Bologna, but he was a foolish man who enjoyed sticking his nose into other people's business. Two persons impressed him above all. They were Bruno and Buffalmaco, two close friends who lived as happily as possible. The physician wondered where they acquired the means to be so happy and carefree. Convinced that they had some secret income, he tried his best to be their friend and succeeded in getting very close to Bruno. He would invite him to dine and chat with him, and the artist would paint different subjects to show his appreciation. Each day Bruno became more and more aware that the physician was a fool.

After some time, Master Simon was confident that he had earned Bruno's familiarity and inquired how he and his friend could afford to live so happily with their modest trade.

"Doctor," Bruno answered, "that is a secret I would not tell anyone. But you are a good friend, and I must confess that with our trade we barely make enough to pay for the water we drink. We get our fun at night because we follow a roving course."

"What is that?" asked the curious physician.

"Oh! I couldn't say without real danger," replied Bruno. Since Master Simon insisted, the artist ended by unveiling the great secret.

A few years before, the wise man Michael Scott had been in Florence. At his departure, he left two of his disciples who were as able as their teacher in necromancy. The two organized a small group of gentlemen and held magic sessions twice a month. During those gatherings, they would follow a roving course. They would not steal like pirates do, but they got whatever they wanted. After they used the desired object, it was returned to the original owner. In this way, they wore splendid garments, enjoyed gilded palaces, slept in sumptuous beds, and lay with famous women. For instance, Bruno

186

would go to bed with the queen of England; Buffalmaco, with the queen of France—two beautiful women, indeed.

The silly physician believed everything he heard and treated the painter with more attention and banquets, hoping to be admitted into the happy group. One night, while Bruno worked on a painting for him, Master Simon confessed that he was in love with a young and beautiful peasant. He had tried to seduce her with gifts to no avail. If he could be a member of the merry company, he might satisfy his desire. Bruno took a long time in answering. Finally he said that it was a truly secret initiation. Every six months, the company's captain and counselors were changed and now Buffalmaco was in line to become the next captain. It was necessary that Simon gain his friendship, for the captain had the power to admit new members after a careful selection.

That gave Buffalmaco a chance to be generously wined and treated by the rich physician. After some time, Master Simon made his request to Buffalmaco. The painter became irked at Bruno for unveiling the secret and started a big fuss. The doctor took all the blame on himself and reconciled the two friends. Little by little, Buffalmaco came to terms and finally promised that he would introduce him at the next meeting. Two conditions were absolute and indispensable: strength to stand the initiation and guts to avoid any mention of God or the saints during the admission trial. Master Simon promised that he could fulfill both conditions.

When the time came, the silly physician was advised to wait during the night on top of a tomb in the cemetery of the Minorite Friars. He wore a scarlet rope and waited for a beast to come and pick him up. Buffalmaco, who was a tall man, wore a frightening mask and donned a black fur. In the dark of that night, he looked like a devilish bear. He went to the cemetery where Master Simon was waiting and made frightening howls and contortions as if he were the very devil. The physician wished he had stayed at home with his wife.

When the beast discharged its rage and grew tame, Master Simon still uncertain, came down from the tomb and mounted the beast, holding his arms crossed on his chest as he had been instructed in advance. Yet, he could not help sighing, "God help me!" He was trembling like a leaf while the beast moved on all fours towards a remote area in the city where some sewer dikes were built for people to empty their vats and collect natural manure for the fields.

The beast ambled there and, with a jerk, tossed the man off its back. He found himself loaded with all kinds of manure, while Buffalmaco and Bruno laughed loudly at a distance.

The second chapter of the physician's troubles started when he went back home and his wife gave him a rough scolding. The third chapter was worse yet. The next morning Bruno and Buffalmaco painted their flesh with livid blotches and went to see the doctor at his house. Everything still smelled bad. They started to call him names because he had betrayed them. He had shown fear and invoked God's name in spite of his solemn pledge. Now they had been beaten like dogs and were in danger of being expelled from the company. Removing their clothes, they showed that they were full of livid marks. The doctor tried to excuse himself, but the two friends had the upper hand. At last, the poor simpleton begged their pardon and tried to appease them the best he could. And if he had so far treated them generously, from then on he entertained them with richer banquets and drinks in order to buy their silence.

# 80. The Duped Whore

It was common in past times that wholesale merchants would transfer their merchandise to a port and deposit it in a warehouse under the supervision of customs agents. These merchants would receive a receipt for the merchandise left in bond and keep the key to the warehouse. The value of the merchandise and other pertinent information was entered in the customs book, and the local brokers informed themselves of each shipment in order to arrange barters and other transactions with the local businessmen.

A young Florentine, Nicholas by name, went to the port of Palermo with a shipment of cloth worth five hundred florins. He deposited his merchandise according to the established procedure and took lodging in town hoping to close a good deal. He was a handsome young man, and since he was not in a hurry to sell, he went about the city looking for some kind of amusement.

A Sicilian lady known as Madame Jancofiore was one of those who thrived by taking advantage of out-of-town merchants. She found out about Nicholas's cargo from a customs broker and started to flirt with him. When she saw he was attracted to her, she sent one of her maids and arranged an appointment in a bathing place.

He went there and was told that the place had been reserved for her. Then two slaves came and cleaned everything carefully. They made a bed with silk linen and luxurious blankets. Afterwards the lady arrived with two more slaves. She met Nicholas with much affection and said, "Nobody could bring me to this but you!" They entered the bath, and she washed him with aromatic soap. Then the two slaves washed Jancofiore and wrapped both lovers in perfumed sheets. After they perspired, the slaves spread pleasant perfumes on the two and left the room. Nicholas thought he was in heaven and enjoyed very much the company of the beautiful Sicilian lady who seemed to be all afire for his love.

From then on, he went to visit her at home and was impressed by the luxury of her residence. Jancofiore was always sugar and honey. The night she heard that Nicholas had sold his merchandise at a good profit, she seemed to melt in his arms.

A couple of days later, Nicholas was again with her. A maid called Jancofiore to a separate room. She returned sometime after weeping in anguish and threw herself on the bed crying aloud. Nicholas wanted to console her and found out, amid her tears and sobs, that she had received sad news. Her brother was condemned to death and she could save his life by depositing a sum of a thousand florins within eight days. She was ready to sell some property and mortgage her belongings, but that would take over two weeks.

Nicholas started to console the grieving lady and told her, "Madame, I can't help you with a thousand florins, but I can lend you five hundred. Luckily I sold my merchandise a short time ago. Had it happened before, I couldn't have lent you a penny."

"Alas!" she cried. "You have been in need of money and didn't tell me. Why didn't you? How can I ask you now?"

Nicholas was taken with these words and brought her the five hundred florins, which she received with her heart full of joy and her eyes full of tears. She assured him that in a couple of weeks she would pay the debt.

Soon after Jancofiore received the money, her sighs of affection started to change. Nicholas wouldn't be received as often as he used to, nor did he enjoy the same caresses as before. The term for the restitution of the money expired several times, and he would get only excuses and alibis. He had no signed document of his loan and at last understood he had been fooled. Unable to do anything, he went to Naples and took counsel with Peter Canigiano, a friend of his who was treasurer to the empress of Constantinople. The shrewd financier heard his story and regretted his vapid simplicity, but he gave him good advice and some money to carry it out.

In a few days Nicholas was back in Palermo with a huge load of bales well-packed and duly fastened, along with a number of oil barrels. He gave the bill of lading to the customs agents and declared the value of his merchandise at two thousand florins. He requested it to be kept in bond until he received the next cargo, worth over three thousand florins.

When the Sicilian vampire saw him back and found out about

Nicholas's rich shipment, she regretted she had aimed at a lower gain and determined to open new channels of communication. She invited him to her home and apologized for her past behavior. She had been promised the sum of the borrowed money from another source, but she could not get it on time. This afflicted her so much that she didn't have the courage to face him. When she did receive her money, he had already left. It was impossible for her to send him the money because he did not give her his new address. She took a purse with five hundred florins, the same she had previously extorted from him, and paid back her debt.

"I hope I did not cause too much annoyance," she concuded.

Nicholas burst into laughter and told her, "Madame, in truth it displeased me somewhat, but I love you so much that I went back home and sold all my possessions to invest in merchandise. I have brought the first shipment here and expect another load worth over three thousand florins. When I receive the whole stock, I'll settle in this town and live close to you."

Jancofiore was very pleased and renewed the fire of her past love. One night, Nicholas came to her house sad and tense.

"Anything wrong?" asked the anxious lady.

"Yes. The boat with my merchandise was captured by pirates. They ask ten thousand florins to release it and the share of my ransom is a thousand florins. They caught me at the moment when I will lose money if I sell the merchandise I have stored in the warehouse."

"I am so sorry," replied the woman. "I wish I had the money to help you. I know a person who helped me with five hundred florins some time ago. But he charges thirty percent and requires collateral for his money. I am ready to mortgage my things for you. How can you assure him of the rest?"

Nicholas guessed her intentions and offered to secure the loan with the merchandise he had in the customs house, provided he could keep the key to show the merchandise to prospective buyers. The deal was agreed upon and the lady disguised the loan with the service of a broker as a middleman.

As soon as Nicholas received the thousand florins, he took off for Naples, repaid Peter Canigiano his money, and thanked him warmly. The beautiful vampire missed Nicholas and after a couple of months started to have doubts about him. Seeing that he did not come back, she had her broker open the warehouse and impound the merchandise. What a surprise! The barrels were filled with water covered with a runlet of oil near the bunghole. The bales were full of tows. And the whole load, worth less than two hundred florins, became quite a burden to carry for a hot mare who had paid in cold cash.

# THE NINTH DAY

## Unrestricted Topics

# 81. The Undesirable Suitors

Madame Francesca was a young and beautiful lady with whom two men, unknown to each other, had fallen in love. At the start, she had unwisely given ear to their entreaties; later, she felt uneasy and tried to withdraw discreetly without showing her true intention.

She found her chance the day a famous criminal died in town and was buried outside the churchyard of the Minorite Friars. She sent word to each of her two suitors. To the first one, Alexander, she said that he would enjoy her favors under one condition. A relative of hers wanted to take the criminal's clothes to her house at night-time. He should go to the tomb, wear the dead man's clothes, and lie flat on the dead body until someone would come and get him. Alexander agreed to do this to prove his courage to the lady.

Then Francesca sent word to the other suitor, Rinuccio, telling him to go and get the buried body and carry it to her house without saying anything of what he heard or felt. Rinuccio agreed to this for her love.

In spite of the frightful mission imposed on them, the two men went separately to do what they were told to do in order to please the capricious lady. Alexander became terrified when he had to undress the dead criminal and wear his clothes. At times he feared that the criminal would rise and kill him. But his ardent love overcame all his fears, and he lay in the tomb awaiting whatever would happen.

At midnight, Rinuccio went to the tomb, resenting that the first request of the woman he loved exposed him to the danger of being caught by the police and being condemned to the fire as a sorcerer. Yet his love was so great that he grabbed the body in the tomb and loaded it on his shoulders. He carried it up to the lady's house, and there she was peeking from the window and scheming how to dismiss both of them with a good excuse.

At that moment, some policemen who were patrolling the street cast the light of their lanterns on Rinuccio approaching the house with Alexander on his shoulders. Immediately, Rinuccio dropped what he thought to be the dead body and ran away. Alexander arose in haste and ran away, too, in spite of the garments hindering him. Both men avoided being arrested. Alexander went home. Rinuccio came back to see if he could find the body and finish his service. The lady went to her bedroom laughing at being loved so much, yet free of any obligation to either.

## 82.  The Sinful Nun

In a famous Lombard convent, there was a young nun, Isabel, who was of noble birth and gifted with extraordinary beauty. One day she fell in love with a gentleman who was accompanying a relative of hers on a visit. The gentleman guessed her intentions and, in time, found a way to have fun with her.

On one occasion, the gentleman was seen by a nun when he was leaving Isabel's cell. The news spread among the other nuns who decided to catch the sinner red-handed before informing the abbess, a highly thought of and pious woman.

A few nights later, the gentleman came back to his lady's cell, and the other nuns who were on the watch formed two groups. One stood at the door of the lovers' room. The other hurriedly went to call the abbess.

Now the abbess happened to be in the company of a priest whom she loved and admitted to the convent in a chest. Afraid that the nuns would break into her room, she dressed in a hurry. In the dark, she caught the priest's breeches instead of her veils and threw them on her head. The nuns were so engrossed in their intention to take Isabel in default that they did not notice what the abbess was wearing.

The group broke the door open and found the two lovers in bed. Isabel was dragged to a chapter meeting, while her lover dressed and went to see how things would proceed. The attention of the nuns was riveted on the guilty lady.

The abbess started her solemn sermon, but the young nun could say nothing to excuse herself. She was so ashamed that many of the other nuns started to feel sorry for her. However, the abbess multiplied her threats. Then Isabel happened to lift her eyes and observe the breeches hanging on the abbess's head. Guessing how the matter stood, she said, "Madame, tie up your coif and then go on."

196

"What coif, you wicked woman?" rejoined the abbess.

"Please tie up your coif and then go on," replied Isabel. The other nuns turned their eyes to the abbess as she touched her head. Everyone in the chapter became aware of the abbess's fault. With feminine quickness, she immediately changed her words and stressed how hard it is to resist the pricks of the flesh. She pleaded to avoid any kind of scandal that would ruin the good reputation of the convent. Isabel went back to bed with her lover—the abbess, with her priest. And the other nuns learned how to push their luck in a more discreet way.

# 83. The Pregnant Man

Calandrino had received a small inheritance from a deceased aunt and decided to purchase an estate with the money. In vain his two astute colleagues, Bruno and Buffalmaco, told him several times to spend some of the money on a banquet. Finally, they talked with another friend, Nello, and decided to have a treat at Calandrino's expense.

The next day, while Calandrino was going to work, Nello greeted him and stared at his face inquisitively. "What's wrong with you, Calandrino? Does anything hurt?" asked Nello.

"What makes you think so?"

"I don't know, but you look so strange to me," remarked the other and went on his way. Not too far off, Buffalmaco met him and asked the same question. Calandrino, who was doubtful at first, now started to worry. Bruno met him soon after and gave the poor man the same tale emphasizing the negative side.

"What shall I do?" asked Calandrino.

"You'd better go home and take care of yourself. You ought to send a specimen of your urine to the doctor. You know that Master Simon is one of our friends."

Downhearted, Calandrino went home straight to bed, convinced that he was sick. Then he sent his specimen to Master Simon, who had his office in the old market area. Bruno, in the meantime, had briefed the physician. Master Simon took the urine and came to see the patient. He felt his pulse while his wife and friends were anxiously waiting for the diagnosis.

"Calandrino," said the physician, after having performed the whole sequence of professional routines, "there is no part of your body that is hurt. You are pregnant."

"Pregnant?" roared Calandrino, turning to his wife. "You wicked woman. This is your doing. For you always like to stay on

198

top, and I had warned you this would happen." His wife blushed for shame, and lowering her head, left the room in silence. Calandrino kept complaining and threatening his wife. Then he started to feel sorry for himself. "Poor me! How shall I deliver the child? I see women make such a painful outcry and they have ample room for it. How can I? I die just at the thought."

While he was complaining, the three friends could hardly conceal their mirth. Master Simon was laughing immoderately. "Don't worry, Calandrino," he said. "I'll make a medicine to take care of your pregnancy. That requires some money, you know."

"Doctor," exclaimed Calandrino, "I put myself in your hands." The doctor sent him a colorful but harmless drink and in three days had his pregnancy cured. Calandrino rose from bed full of joy, and his friends enjoyed a rich banquet out of the medical fee paid by the fooled chap.

## 84.   An Ungrateful Swindler

Two gentlemen from Siena, Angiolieri and Fortarrigo, were close friends. Their manners were quite different, but on one thing they fully agreed: both men hated intensely their own fathers. Angiolieri, unhappy with the allowance he received, decided to better his lot by serving the pope's legate. He convinced his father to give him an advance on his allowance and bought himself new clothes and a horse.

Once his friend Fortarrigo heard about Angiolieri's new goal, he besought him to hire him as a lackey. Angiolieri told him that he trusted his ability to serve, but had no intention of hiring him for two reasons—he was a gambler and a drinker. Fortarrigo made all kinds of entreaties. Finally he was hired.

Both men set out and stopped to eat at noon during their journey. Angiolieri took a siesta after dinner, but his lackey went immediately to the tavern where he had a few drinks and couldn't resist the temptation of gambling. There he lost his money and even his clothes. He returned to Angiolieri's room in his shirt and found the master asleep. His attention was caught by a purse full of money. He took the entire amount, went back to gamble, and lost that, too.

When Angiolieri woke up, he dressed and decided to leave his drunken friend behind, replacing him with a more trustworthy servant. But trouble started when he went to pay the innkeeper and found no money. He cried out that he had been robbed. While he threatened to have everyone arrested, Fortarrigo came back in his shirt to get his master's clothes and continue gambling with them.

"My clothes are in pawn for thirty-eight francs," he said. "I am sure he will return them for thirty-five."Angiolieri found out that his servant had had a big loss and started to threaten him. The other would only reply that he could get back his clothes for thirty-five francs if he paid the amount at once. Angiolieri lost his patience, mounted his horse, and left irritated, among other reasons, by some people's suspicion that he had given Fortarrigo his money for gambling. While he rode away, the other followed him insisting with the same refrain: "My clothes are worth thirty-eight francs, but I can get them back for thirty-five if I pay now."

These words were obsessing him. Angiolieri spurred his horse and rode faster. Fortarrigo saw a group of workers ahead and yelled at them to stop the rider as if he were a thief, which they did. In vain, Angiolieri tried to tell them the truth. The other reached him and, with the help of those workers, stripped him of his clothes and rode off on his horse. Then he spread the rumor that he had won the horse and clothes gambling at the tavern with Angiolieri, who had to suffer both the loss and the mockery.

## 85. Framed-up Lover

Calandrino, together with his colleagues Bruno, Buffalmaco, and Nello was painting the country house of a rich gentleman, whose bachelor son, Philip, used to bring some girls there to have fun. While the four painters were working, Philip brought a loose woman called Niccolosa. One day, she was drawing water from the well, and Calandrino came there for the same purpose. The poor simpleton looked odd to her, so she treated him with a strange familiarity. He thought that he had attracted her and quickly fancied a love adventure. His colleague, Bruno, heard his sighs and got his confidence. "She might be Philip's wife," he remarked. "Let's hope Buffalmaco perceives nothing."

"I don't worry about Buffalmaco," answered Calandrino. "I am rather leery of Nello, because he is my wife's relative and might spoil everything."

Bruno agreed with Calandrino, but resolved to fool him because he already knew that Niccolosa was a call girl. He made arrangements with her and her lover, and later on went to visit them with his friend. The woman exchanged conspicuous signs of passion with Calandrino while Philip seemed to be blind to their grimaces. Bruno swore that she was in love with the gullible painter and told him to take his guitar the next day and court her more actively. All this caused more fun and merriment among the whole group.

There was a constant exchange of sighs going on, winking of eyes and other exaggerated gestures between the woman and Calandrino, but nothing concrete ever happened. The poor man was anxious to achieve his goal and asked Bruno for a final push.

"Simple," replied Bruno. "Would you touch her with a script I'll give you?"

"Sure!" answered Calandrino.

"Bring me a virgin parchment, a bat, three grains of incense,

202

and a blessed candle," said Bruno. 'I'll take care of the rest."

Calandrino spent the night chasing a bat and, finally, brought it to Bruno who wrote a script on the parchment with its blood. In the meantime, Nello went to inform Calandrino's wife that he was about to betray her. She became blind with jealousy, took a maid along, and went to the place indicated.

Once the other men were sure that the wife was coming, they all agreed to give a final touch to the adventure. Philip said that he was going back to Florence on business, while he actually went to hide in a place from where he could see everything. Niccolosa went to the courtyard and waited alone. Bruno gave the parchment with the magic script to Calandrino, who went to Niccolosa and, after a few amenities, touched her with it. She followed him to the barn. As soon as they were inside, she closed the door, grabbed him by the arms, and threw him on the straw. Then, holding his hands behind him, she mounted astride him and started to recite a long amorous tirade.

Suddenly, the door of the barn opened. The jealous wife rushed in fuming and battered her aroused husband. Niccolosa ran away. Calandrino's friends came in on time to rescue the bruised victim and stop the scandal.

## 86.  Sex Orgy in the Dark

A poor but good man lived with his beautiful wife in a small house in the countryside. They had two children: a teenage daughter, who was a very appealing girl, and a little son not yet one year old. Due to the location of the house, quite a few travelers stopped there to eat and drink, and the poor man made his money with this business. It happened that a gentleman named Pinuccio was attracted to the teenage girl and loved her ardently. The girl was proud of his attention, and both lovers were anxious to satisfy their desires.

One evening, Pinuccio arrived at the girl's house with his friend Adrian, pretending to have just returned from another town. It was too late for them to reach Florence, so they asked the good man to let them spend the night in his small house. The host recognized them and gave them hospitality, apologizing for the lack of comfort and space in the house. As a matter of fact, after they took care of the horses and had supper, the host and his wife went to the only bedroom in the house and arranged the three available beds at three different corners in the room. The two gentlemen were put to sleep in one bed. After they had supposedly fallen asleep, the young daughter was sent to sleep in another bed. Then the good man with his wife occupied the third bed, while the child was placed in a cradle beside their bed.

Pinuccio memorized the arrangements of the beds and, after everyone was sleeping, he went to join the girl. She received him joyfully, for she felt protected by the dark. While the two young folks were spending the best night of their lives, a cat knocked something over and the noise awoke the mother. In the dark, she got up, pushed the cradle aside, and went out to check what the noise was. In the meantime, Adrian had to run to the bathroom. He stumbled over the cradle on his way and pushed it alongside his bed. When he came back to his bed, he forgot to set the cradle where it belonged.

204

The good wife, having found nothing wrong, groped her way back to her bed. But the cradle was not there, and she suddenly moved away, afraid to make a mistake. Then she entered the bed near which the cradle was set and rested in full assurance of being with her husband. Actually she was with Adrian, who not yet asleep received her in his arms to no small contentment of the unaware lady.

Meanwhile, Pinuccio left the girl and went back to his bed. Again, the cradle stood in the way, and Pinuccio thought he had gotten lost in the dark. So he entered the other bed, waking up the sleeping man. Convinced that the man was his friend Adrian, he told him he had had the greatest fun in the world with the host's daughter. "I have gone," he said, "upwards of six times to the country since I left you in bed."

"What in the world is he doing here?" wondered the host. Then he became incensed and started to threaten Pinuccio, who had lost control of the situation.

"What's the matter with our guests?" wondered the wife, sure that her bed partner was her husband.

"Forget about them," answered Adrian laughing. "They had too many last night."

The good wife, hearing the stranger's voice in her bed, immediately realized what had happened. Without saying a word, she grabbed the cradle with the little child and went to lie in her daughter's bed. The noise became louder, and she asked her husband what was wrong.

"Haven't you heard what he said about our daughter?"

"He lies through his throat," said the woman. "I haven't been able to close an eye during the night and have rested here with my daughter. You men drink too much and don't know what you say. In any case, why is Pinuccio in bed with you?"

Adrian, seeing how adroitly the lady had covered the double scandal, called his friend back. "Pinuccio, come back here. The devil with your sleepwalking! You dream of nonsense and talk of it freely. Come back here."

The host heard both his wife and Adrian talk and believed the young man was dreaming. He shook Pinuccio's shoulders and told him to wake up. Pinuccio played his part properly and went back to his bed.

The next day, the host kept mocking Pinuccio for his funny dreams, but the young man found other means to carry on his affair with the girl. As for her, she always vowed to her mother that she had not lain with Pinuccio, who must have been dreaming the things he said. The good wife remembered well Adrian's grip and figured that she alone had waked during that odd night.

## 87.  A Suspicious Wife

Talano Molese was a pious man who had married Margaret, a beautiful young lady, but ill-tempered and displeasing. One night, Talano dreamed that his wife was walking in the woods and a fierce wolf attacked her throat. She was barely saved from the beast, but her looks were marred forever. When he woke up, he told her not to go out to the woods on account of his bad dream.

The wicked woman made some negative comments about her husband's bad dream, but promised not to go out. After he left, she became suspicious and did exactly the opposite. She went to the woods expecting to catch her husband involved in some immoral traffic. While she was spying around without any thought of danger, a terrible wolf jumped out and grabbed her by the throat, carrying her away like a lamb. Luckily, some shepherds encountered the running wolf and saved her from mortal danger.

The physicians saved her life, but not her looks. From then on, the ill-natured wife lived more troubled than ever and stayed continuously inside from shame of being seen.

## 88.   The Revenge of a Glutton

Ciacco was the greatest glutton who ever lived in Florence. His means were not enough to support his gluttony, but he found a way to satisfy it. He was a man full of pleasant sayings and humor, which made his company likable to many rich men who delighted in banquets and drinking parties. There was also in Florence a dandy called Biondello who plied the same trade as Ciacco.

One morning Biondello was coming from the market with two fresh lampreys. Ciacco saw him and asked what he was going to do with those fish.

"Master Corso Donati has received three more lampreys and a sturgeon," said Biondello. "He is going to have a dinner with some gentlemen. Are you coming?"

"Of course," replied Ciacco. And he arrived punctually at Corso Donati's house to find that there was no banquet at all. At dinner time, only chick-peas and a dish of fried fish were served. Ciacco ate without any appetite because he saw himself scorned by his colleague. Inwardly, he swore to avenge himself of this mockery.

Without wasting any time, Ciacco hired an astute huckster and showed him a tall gentleman who was famous in Florence for his arrogance and authority. The name of this choleric nobleman was Philip Argenti. Ciacco gave the huckster a big empty bottle and told him to approach Master Philip Argenti carefully and say to him, "Sir, Biondello sends you this flask for some of your good wine to entertain some friends of his." Due to Philip Argenti's bad temper, Ciacco recommended his man to be on his guard and avoid falling into the nobleman's rawboned hands. He would be paid after carrying out his services, which he did.

Later on Ciacco informed Biondello that Master Philip Argenti was looking for him at the Gallery. Curious to find out why, Biondello went where the nobleman was still fuming with rage. As soon as

Biondello approached the angry man, he grabbed him by the hair and cast him to the ground, unloading blows and insults on his face and ribs. At last, some bystanders dragged the poor victim away from the enraged man.

On his way home, Biondello met Ciacco who asked him laughingly, "How did you like Master Argenti's wine?"

"I wish Master Corso's lampreys had tasted the same to you!" answered Biondello. And from then on, a long truce was kept between the two parasites.

# 89. Solomon's Advice

In old times, King Solomon was famous for his wisdom in deciding his people's business. Two men with different problems came to consult with the king. One was Melissus, a very rich young man who spent a fortune by entertaining his fellow townsmen without ever receiving a token of their affection. The other was Joseph, who was on his way to Solomon's court because he couldn't handle his perverse and frivolous wife any longer.

Each one of them was admitted to the king's presence. To Melissus, Solomon said, "Love!" To Joseph, the unhappy husband, he counseled, "Go to Goosebridge."

The two men went away rather disappointed with the royal advice and made their return journey together. At one point, they came to a river with a fine bridge. A caravan of horses and mules was crossing it, and both Joseph and Melissus waited aside for them to pass. It happened that a mule from the caravan took umbrage and refused to pass on. The owner tried all means to push his beast and finally had to grab a stick to force the animal with heavy blows. Our two travelers tried to calm down the incensed muleteer, but he answered that he knew his mule and kept on hitting until he reached his purpose. Before starting to cross the bridge, Joseph asked for the name of that place and was told, "Goosebridge."

"Now I see that Solomon's advice starts to make sense," said Joseph to his fellow traveler. After a few days, he arrived at his home town and invited Melissus to be his guest. He accepted, and Joseph took him home and told his wife to prepare a meal according to his guest's wishes. Of course, the unsympathetic wife did just the opposite.

"Was that the meal you were told to prepare?" asked Joseph firmly.

"So what?" answered his wife with a laugh. "I did it as I pleased.

Take it or leave it."

Joseph went to get a solid stick and grabbed the moaning wife by the hair. At first, she started to threaten him, then to beg and entreat. But the angry husband kept on dispensing his furious blows until there was not a spot left unbruised on her body. Then he joined his friend Melissus and said, "Tomorrow we'll see the effects of the Goosebridge advice." As a matter of fact, the next day the beaten wife got up on time and worked hard to please him and his guest.

Melissus left for his town and found out that the advice he received from Solomon was just as correct as the one given to Joseph. He started to love his fellow citizens and they reciprocated the feeling, for love is a contagious experience.

## 90.  The Interrupted Enchantment

Dom John Barolo was the pastor of a very poor parish. To make ends meet, he used to load his horse with merchandise and trade it. During one of his frequent trips, he met another trades-man—Peter Tresanti—who was poor and had just married a young and buxom wife. The two part-time merchants would host each other during their trips. When Dom John came to Tresanti's house, for lack of space he spread some straw in the stable and lay on it. The young wife felt sorry for the poor priest and offered to sleep at her girl friend's house, but the priest refused to inconvenience the young couple in spite of her insistence.

"Never mind about me," said the priest one night. "I fare better than you think. At night, I say a certain charm and change my mare into a beautiful woman. In the morning she becomes again a mare, and I go on with my business."

The young wife was intrigued and pressed her husband to con-vince the priest to do them the same favor. During the day, she would become a mare to help him carry more merchandise. At night, she would be again his wife. That would help them get ahead.

The priest listened to his credulous host with malicious interest and promised to teach him how to change his wife into a mare pro-vided that he observe every detail of his demonstration. Neither he nor his wife were supposed to utter a word, otherwise they would spoil everything.

That very night, the young wife undressed herself and stood on all fours, expecting to be changed into a mare. The astute priest passed his hand over her face and head. "Be this a fine mare's face and mane," he said. Then he caressed her arms bidding that they be a fine mare's legs and hoofs. The same he did with her chest, awak-ening at that point the feeler hidden under his long shirt. Likewise he went on with her back, belly, and legs. Finally only the tail was to be made. He quickly lifted up his shirt and pushed his man-planting dibble into the appropriate fur. "And this be a fine mare's tail!" exclaimed the priest.

"Hold it!" yelled the simpleminded husband.

"Too bad!" concluded the priest. "The mare was all but made, but your words destroyed everything forever."

"Why didn't you ask me to set the tail on her?" asked the disillusioned husband.

"You wouldn't know how," objected the priest.

The young woman was disappointed at her husband and resented his intrusion. Poor Peter went on trading his modest goods with his usual donkey.

# THE TENTH DAY

## Generous and Chivalric Deeds

## 91. The Unrewarded Knight

King Alfonso of Spain was superior to the other sovereigns of Europe in his bravery and generosity. Many knights would go to his court where they were honored with gifts and other rewards. Roger Figiovanni, a rich and high-spirited Tuscan knight, lived for some time at Alfonso's court, but was systematically ignored by the king. Seeing himself forgotten in spite of his marvelous deeds of arms, he decided to leave. The king gave him a mule and told one of his servants to follow him one full day and report back to him whatever Roger would say.

Both men journeyed together. At a certain point, they reached a river where they watered their horses. The mule refused to budge from the middle of the stream. "The devil with you," exclaimed the knight. "You are made after the king who gave you to me."

The next day, the monarch had been informed of his reaction and recalled Roger to his court asking him why he had said those words.

"Majesty," replied Roger, "I likened the mule to you because she stalled where she shouldn't have, and vice versa."

"Roger," said the king, "if I have given much to people far below your merits and neglected you, it is fortune that should be blamed. And I'll prove it to you." Then he showed Roger two locked coffers and told him to choose one for himself. Roger did and, when he opened it, he found it full of sand.

"That's your luck!" said the king. "The other was full of gold and precious jewels." He opened it, saying to Roger, "I know you don't want to become a Spanish subject and therefore I shall bestow no castle or city on you. Yet I want you to have this precious coffer that fortune took away from you." Roger received the coffer joyfully and returned home.

## 92.  The Dieting Abbot

The abbot of Cluny was one of the richest dignitaries in the Catholic Church. Because of stomach trouble, the physicians prescribed he take the mineral baths in Siena. He went there escorted by a large group of servants and many defenders. Before reaching the city, they had to cross some territory infested with dangerous bandits, led by Ghino of Tacco. This latter ambushed the powerful abbot and his knights in a straight passage and sent a messenger requesting them to surrender. The prelate was furious and brandished all his excommunications and interdicts, but surrendered when he saw that he and his men were in a trap.

Ghino accommodated the large group of men in comfortable quarters at his castle, but lodged the powerful monk in a small, dark room. Unknown as he was to the abbot, he went to him and asked, "Ghino should like to know where you are going and why." The other laid aside his pride and gave all the information requested by his attendant.

The next day, he went back to the abbot and said, "Sir, Ghino has studied medicine and recommends a light diet." He left only two slices of bread and a glass of wine for his meals, and that did not make the prelate too happy. The abbot asked to see Ghino and was assured that his message would be delivered.

For a few days, Ghino kept the abbot on his rigid diet until he saw that he had eaten some dry beans he secretly left around the room. Then he told the monk, "Sir, you are healed, and it is time for you to leave the clinic." The other was happy to come out of that narrow room.

A few days later, he admitted that he was completely recovered from his stomach ailment. Then Ghino confessed that it was bad luck and the persecution of his political enemies that led him to be a highway robber. "Now that I have cured your stomach ailment," he added, "you are free to go. I will not touch any of your rich belongings, but you are free to leave anything you wish for my services."

The powerful prelate was delighted to find that the man who had served him was Ghino, and he forgot all his previous anger, admiring such a generous gesture. He wanted to become Ghino's friend and left many gifts for him.

Once in Rome, he asked the pope for a grace and he received it. He begged him to forgive Ghino who had wrongly been outlawed, and pleaded for him to be joined to the cause of the Church. The pope called Ghino to the court and noticed that he was a brave and worthy man. Therefore, he made him a knight and gained a faithful servant.

## 93. The Two Philanthropists

In ancient times, Nathan, a very rich and noble man, possessed a castle located close to the highway between East and West. His soul was so generous that no person would go through his place without being honorably received and entertained. His praiseworthy hospitality made his name famous throughout many countries.

Nathan was already aged when his fame reached Mithridanes, who was as rich and eager to surpass everybody else in liberality. Accordingly, he built a sumptuous palace and received all transient people with lavish manners.

Once there came a poor woman to ask for alms, and he treated her well. She came to his gate day after day for twelve days. The thirteenth day, Mithridanes lost his patience and berated her.

"Oh, for the liberality of Nathan!" she exclaimed. "I went through each of his thirty-two gates, and he always gave to me without bothering to recognize me. And here I have been recognized at the thirteenth gate."

At the old woman's remark, Mithridanes felt very bad. He grew jealous of Nathan, who had obscured the glory of his liberality. He felt so jealous that he decided to kill the old man. Taking a good supply of money to carry out his irrational purpose, he arrived at his rival's castle and found old Nathan unattended while taking a walk. Mithridanes asked him if he could inform him where Nathan lived. The old man said that nobody could do that better than he. They both went together to the palace, and Nathan told his servants to take good care of the young guest without telling him that he was Nathan. To satisfy Mithridanes's curiosity, Nathan said he was an old servant in the palace, who had known the owner well since childhood. "He never advanced me, and I owe him no gratitude." These words endeared the old man to Mithridanes, and the two men became close friends.

One day, the assumed servant asked him what brought him to that part of the country, and Mithridanes hesitantly resolved to tell him everything about his plan after asking for a pledge of secrecy. Nathan, hearing such a cruel purpose, was inwardly upset. Nevertheless, he answered with a calm countenance and told him that Nathan used to take a walk along the coppice. "If you decide to slay him, turn to your left and follow that road. It is safer than the one you took in coming here."

Mithridanes put his plan into effect the next morning. But before killing his unknown rival, he decided to talk to him. He jumped on the old man and grabbed him by the hair at the back of his head.

"Nathan, you are dead," he shouted.

"Then I have deserved it," the old man answered.

Mithridanes, recognizing his voice, turned the man's face to him and felt his rage changed into shame. He threw away his sword and knelt at Nathan's feet, avowing the greatness of his rival's liberality.

Nathan raised him to his feet and tenderly embraced him. "Son," he said, "very little is left of my life, and by giving it away don't think I am generous. Neither feel so ashamed, because you aimed at glory by killing just one man, while kings and emperors destroy a great number of lives and burn entire countries for the same purpose."

Mithridanes was amazed at the greatness of old Nathan and commended his noble soul. Yet, he could not explain how he dared to face the great danger of which he was fully aware.

"Son," replied the old man, "my nature is to give anything I have to anyone who comes and asks for it. You came for my life, and if you wanted it, I would satisfy your wish, thinking that this would be the proper way to end it. After all, sooner or later, I'll lose it and I doubt there will ever be another chance for me to find someone else who makes a request of my life. Again, take it if you so wish."

"God forbid!" exclaimed Mithridanes. "I wish I could add my own life to increase yours!"

"You really mean it?" asked Nathan.

"I really do," answered the other.

"Then take all my possessions and take my name, and I'll go to your house and call myself Mithridanes. Young as you are, you can keep my name alive and glorious for a long time."

"If I knew how to bear your name with the same glory as you do, I would not hesitate for a second. But I am afraid I couldn't live up to it and would mar the fame you have gained."

After these words they departed from each other with reciprocal affection and respect.

## 94.  The Discreet Lover

A young nobleman, Gentil Carisendi, fell in love with Madame Catalina, the wife of a respected gentleman. In spite of his sincere love, Gentil received nothing in return from the lady. The frustrated lover was appointed to a high position in the justice department of a nearby town and left. Meanwhile the lady, who was pregnant, went to a country house and decided to live there during a rather long absence of her husband. Attacked by a sudden illness, she lost all signs of life and was declared dead by the physicians. Her relatives buried her without making any attempt at saving the child she bore since she had not been pregnant very long.

Gentil heard about the death of the woman he loved so dearly and was deeply grieved. In despair, he decided to go and see her dead, since he never could enjoy her alive. He took her out of her tomb and kissed her face tenderly. Then he felt a strange urge to touch her breast, and there he perceived a faint beat of her heart. Putting aside the first wave of fear, he took her home, where his old mother brought the unfortunate lady back to life and took care of her. She asked to be sent back home. Gentil offered to do it under some simple conditions: that is, he would give her back in a solemn banquet after she was in perfect shape again.

Under the care of Gentil's mother, she recovered and later on had a lovely child. The new mother grew healthier each day and looked unusually beautiful. Gentil respected her honorable wishes and treated her like a sister. One day, he gathered a group of distinguished citizens, among whom was Catalina's husband.

He told her what he meant to do. During the banquet he presented a hypothetical situation and asked his guests for advice. A gentleman had a servant who became very sick. The master lost all hopes that he would survive and abandoned him on the street. Another man took him home and brought him back to health. The

222

former master went to claim his servant, but the second refused to return him. Was he right in doing so?

The gentlemen debated the issue and, at last, committed the response to the allegedly-dead lady's husband, who agreed that the servant belonged to the new master. Almost everyone concurred with such a decision, and Gentil was highly gratified with it. Then he promised to follow a Persian tradition whereby the host presents his guests with the most precious thing he has in the world. He called in the lady with her child, both elegantly dressed. The gentlemen paid her the utmost honor and admired her beauty and manners. They asked her different questions, but she answered none. Since the guests became very curious, Gentil told them that she was the servant he had mentioned earlier. And in an orderly way he started to repeat the story of his unfortunate love and his wish to give the first and last kiss to the dead body with the happy ending there visible.

"Nicholas," he concluded, addressing the lady's husband by name, "if you haven't changed your mind, the lady is mine."

Everyone heard his words with compassion and a feeling of suspense. Gentil rose to his feet and took the child in his arms. "Stand up, Nicholas," he said to the lady's husband. "This is your son. I am his godfather. And take back your wife, who has lived chastely in my mother's house." The husband was happy to receive her back with the child, while Gentil earned unanimous praise.

## 95. Magic and Love

Madame Dianora, the wife of a rich gentleman called Gilbert, was a woman full of charm. A noble and great baron, Hansald Gradense, fell in love with her and tried in all possible ways to encourage her to respond to his feelings. The honest lady refused all his messages and, finally, made an impossible condition in order to get rid of him. She would accept his love only if he could have a garden full of blooming flowers during the frigid month of January. If he could not produce such a garden, he was to stop bothering her, for she would inform her husband and relatives of his approaches.

When Hansald heard such a condition, he understood the true motive of Madame Dianora. Yet, impelled by his great love, he decided to leave nothing untried. He sent messengers in all directions until he found a man who had mastered magic. For a large sum of money, the necromant promised to produce the garden on January first of the next year.

On January first, a beautiful meadow full of blooming flowers appeared close to the city while the rest of the countryside was covered by snow and ice. Hansald collected a bunch of flowers and fruits and sent them secretly to Madame Dianora to remind her of her promise.

Faced with this prodigious event, the lady began to repent of her promise and felt very badly. She couldn't help telling her husband the cause of her anguish. The husband pointed out how unwise it was to even listen to another man's proposals, but he bet on her chastity under any conditions. Yet, he understood her pure intentions and authorized her to keep her word. It was up to her suitor to absolve her from her promise.

Heartbroken, the lady with her maid went to Hansald's house early in the morning. He received her with reverence and respect. Then he asked her the reason for coming so early and in such company.

"Sir," she answered, "neither love nor faith to the given word brings me here, but my husband's wish. He has more regard for your disorderly passion than for his own honor."

Hansald was moved by her husband's generosity and felt his love change into compassion. Therefore he freed her from her promise and told her to give sincere thanks to her man. The necromancer was highly impressed both by the lover's noble reaction and the husband's unselfishness. When Hansald offered to pay him the huge sum they had agreed upon, he refused to accept it. "Since I have seen you liberal in your love and the husband in his honor, I shall be liberal in my services," he said. And there was no way to have him take even a small sum.

# 96. The Ashamed King

King Charles the First, after his victory in the war against King Manfred, started to rule over the kingdom of Naples. One day he heard that a gentleman, named Neri, had the most beautiful gardens in town. Since Neri belonged to the opposite party, the king decided to gain him for his cause. So he sent Neri word that he wished to have supper in his gardens together with four dignitaries. Neri made magnificent preparations to receive the king. When he came, he expressed his appreciation for the gardens and then took a seat at the table arranged close to a crystal-clear fish pond.

Two teenage twin girls with golden hair and angelical faces joined the group and made a curtsey before the king. One of them, carrying a net, plunged into the pond, started to catch fish, and cast them to the other sister who fried them and served the king. At times, he would catch the fish cast by the girl and throw them back into the water. In this fashion, they frolicked a while until the meal was ready.

The girls, seeing that the fish were cooked, passed shyly before the king, their delicate garments adhering to the skin of their perfect bodies. Then they returned home. The gentlemen commended both the physical beauty of the girls and their agreeable manners. The king was highly impressed with them and felt a strange attraction. When he asked who they were, the host answered that they were his twin daughters and their names were Guinevere and Iseult the Blonde. At the end of the meal, both sisters, dressed in elegant garments, came again bringing two platters full of fruit. They served the guests and sang some carols to entertain them. The king felt more and more attracted to Guinevere, and before long found himself to be in love with her. From then on he didn't miss a chance to get closer to Neri in order to see Guinevere.

At last, unable to repress his passion, King Charles revealed his desire to possess the girl to Count Guy. The good count was amazed and answered very frankly. How could he, in his mature years, do something he never thought of at a younger age? He had just invaded an unknown kingdom, and the turmoil derived from such a scandal would create a wave of hatred among the new subjects. Moreover, this was not the way to appreciate the kind hospitality of a gentleman who had previously belonged to the opposite party. He would be considered a wolf rather than a monarch. "Let me tell you," concluded Count Guy. "It was a great victory for you to win King Manfred. But your greatest victory will be to conquer yourself and curb your appetites."

The king understood the wise advise given by Count Guy and, with Neri's agreement, married the two beautiful girls to two outstanding gentlemen in his court. Then he took a long vacation, and with continuous exercise and fatigue, he vexed the fierce prick of his passion until he was left free of his dishonest desire.

## 97.  The Commoner and the King

When the population of Sicily revolted against French domina-
tion, King Pedro of Aragon came to help them with his army. To
celebrate the ensuing victory, he held splendid tournaments in Palermo with his barons. Lisa, the daughter of an apothecary, saw the
king from her window and was impressed so much by his gallant
manners that she fell in love with him. She realized her low condition
and saw no way for her dream to come true. Under such pressure,
she became ill and was slowly fading in spite of the medical assistance and affectionate care supplied by her parents.

Aware that her sickness would drive her to death, she decided
to tell the king of her love before she died. She asked her father to
call for Minuccio, a famous minstrel who sang and performed before
the sovereign.

When Minuccio came, she wanted to be alone with him. She
told him what an unfortunate girl she was to aim so high. Only death
was the final reward she could expect for her love. Since she was
ready to die, her last consolation would be to know that the king had
been informed of her feelings.

Minuccio marveled at the greatness of her soul and felt deep
compassion for her. He promised to oblige her in a few days. He
went to a friend of his who was a poet, and had a beautiful poem
composed about Lisa's hopeless love. Then he put it to music, and
the final outcome was an inspiring song that he sang at court. Such
was the intensity of his feelings that the song was a sudden hit. Even
the king was so touched that he wanted to know its origin. Minuccio
said that he would tell him alone, and King Pedro listened to Lisa's
sad story in a private audience with the minstrel. Having compassion
for such a worthy damsel, the king promised to go and see her that
very evening.

Minuccio brought the good news to Lisa, and the poor girl immediately showed signs of improvement. The king was a generous prince and a compassionate man. In the evening, he went to ask the girl's father to show him the garden of his house. The apothecary was amazed to see him in his own house and tried to entertain him as best he could.

During the visit, King Pedro asked the apothecary about his daughter and inquired whether she was still single or married. Since the poor father replied that she was very sick, he expressed his wish to see the girl whose beauty he remembered well. The father took him to her chamber.

"What is this, my lady?" asked the king, taking her by the hand. "You are young and should comfort other ladies, yet you let yourself down. For our love, take care of your health and make a quick recovery."

"My lord," replied Lisa, carried to the heaven of sudden happiness. "My will to subject my little strength to such a heavy burden has caused this sickness. Thanks to your goodness, I shall be fine very soon."

The king understood her covert speech and consoled her for a while. A few days later, Lisa felt sustained by her hope and recovered at a fast pace.

The king took counsel with the queen as to what he should do with such a love. One day the royal couple and many other noble people went to visit Lisa and her parents. After they solaced themselves, King Pedro called Lisa before the queen and said, "Noble young lady, we are honored by your great love and therefore we feel like giving you a token of our appreciation. Since you are ready for marriage, we should like you to marry a gentleman we bestow on you under the condition that we receive only one kiss from you and that we be considered your knight."

The girl became red with shame and replied in a low voice that she was aware that people would consider it a crazy idea that the daughter of Bernard the apothecary would address the ardor of her soul to so high a personage. For the love of him, she not only would marry whomever he decided, but would throw herself into the flames. She was flattered to have him as her knight. As for the kiss, the only token of her love, she said she could not deliver it without the queen's permission.

229

Her answer pleased the queen, who found her as discreet as the king had described her. Then he announced his decision to Lisa's parents, who were highly delighted to have their daughter married to a nobleman designated by His Majesty. King Pedro took Lisa's head in his hands and kissed her tenderly on her forehead. From then on, he always called himself her knight and, whenever he went to any deed of arms, he carried the sign received from her. By so doing, King Pedro knew how to gain the hearts of his new subjects.

## 98. The Replaced Husband

Titus Quintus Fulvius was a young man belonging to one of the most powerful families in ancient Rome. His father sent him to study in Greece. Here he was the guest in the house of a noble Greek who had a son of the same age. The two young folks, Titus and Gisippus, became very close friends and enjoyed each other's company as if they were members of the same home. As a matter of fact, when the old man died, they both regretted his death as if he were their common father.

A few months after that sad circumstance, family and friends advised Gisippus to take a wife, and he found for himself a young and beautiful lady from Athens, called Sophronia. One day Gisippus took his friend Titus to see his fiancée. Titus liked Sophronia very much and in a short time found himself in love with the young lady. Yet he could not bring himself to accept the fact that he should fall in love with the woman betrothed to his best friend. This caused a crisis which each day grew worse and worse.

Gisippus, perceiving his friend weak and sickly looking, tried to assist him as best he could. Titus told him several idle tales and, at last, found the courage to express the true reason of his malaise, stating in tears that he would prefer death to the baseness into which he had fallen. Gisippus stood undecided for a while. He was taken by the girl's charms, but was far from being desperately in love with her. Glad that Titus had not hidden the truth, he accepted as a natural thing the fact that his friend had fallen in love with Sophronia. But the engagement was settled. Breaking it at such a stage would lose the girl for both of them. Therefore Gisippus, in the name of their friendship, proposed to go on with the planned marriage, but he would not sleep with her as a wife. Since Titus desired her more, he would stay in the bedroom with her.

The more Gisippus was liberal, the more his friend felt ashamed and guilty, but his love was so great that in the end he accepted the deal. By this time, he recovered his health and good humor.

After the wedding was duly celebrated, Gisippus took the young bride to his bedroom and dousing all the lights, went to the next room where his friend was resting. He told him to go to bed with Sophronia. Titus felt overcome by shame and guilt, but Gisippus was determined to fulfill his friend's pleasure and pushed him into the bride's chamber. He took her in his arms and in a whisper asked her if she wanted to be his wife.

"Yes," replied Sophronia, unaware of the change of men.

"And I want to be your husband," said Titus, setting a precious ring on her finger.

Soon after, Titus lost his father in Rome and decided to go back to be in charge of his family's fortune. Therefore, both friends decided to inform Sophronia of what had taken place. The girl listened to their story in a state of shock and felt cheated. Weeping bitterly, she ran away to her parents' home. This started a scandal, and Gisippus was held in contempt both by his and Sophronia's relatives.

During a rough confrontation between both families, reasoning brought no results. Titus listened to their noisy complaints and menaces with no little annoyance. Having a Roman spirit and Greek wit, he adroitly chose the right moment and place to give them an answer. He emphasized the laws of love and friendship. Then he analyzed the case. They had given Sophronia to a noble man, and he was very noble. They had given her to a learned young man, and he was learned, too. They had given her to a Greek and he was a Roman. So what? Wasn't Rome the greatest republic in those times? Wasn't he a member of a powerful family in Rome? What else did they expect?

"I know," he concluded, "that you liked to have Gisippus as a kinsman in Athens, but you will not have me less dear in Rome as a patron of public interest and private needs. I hope you need not experience the spite of a noble Roman soul."

Sophronia's relatives clearly understood the covert allusion of the powerful Roman and gave him back the girl as his legitimate wife. He took her to Rome, where they lived happily.

But Gisippus was held in contempt by everybody, and some time later he was exiled in poverty. Dejected and poorly dressed, he went to Rome and stopped at Titus' house. Titus happened to pass by and failed to recognize him. Gisippus felt shunned and departed in despair. It was night, and he went to sleep in a cave.

Early in the morning, two thieves took refuge in the same cave. The scoundrels had an argument about sharing the booty they had stolen, and one of them slew the other and ran away. Hoping to find death, Gisippus stood near the murdered thief and waited for the police to come and blame him for the killing.

He was sentenced to death. The day that he was being brought to the execution place, Titus saw his face and recognized his old and dear friend. Anxious to help him, he had no other means but to blame himself for the death that had occurred in the cave. Gisippus felt touched by Titus' abnegation and insisted that he was the true murderer.

The judge was intrigued by the new circumstance. He searched for some technicality to acquit both of them when a man came from the crowd, a man notorious as a rogue, who confessed the truth that he had killed his partner while Gisippus was sleeping in the cave. That was enough to excuse both friends. Sophronia received Gisippus at home just like a brother. Some time later, he took the Roman citizenship and became a part of the family by marrying Titus's unwed sister.

# 99. Timely Return

In the days of Emperor Frederick the First, a general crusade was undertaken against Saladin who ruled the Holy Land. This valiant king wanted to have a firsthand account of the Christian armies and therefore, disguised as a merchant, resolved to visit some European strategic center.

One night, Saladin was traveling on the road from Milan to Pavia with a small group of trusted officers also disguised as merchants. There they met an Italian gentleman, Torello by name, and asked for a place where they might find lodging. Torello, impressed by their manners, lodged them in his country castle and entertained them as best he could. Then he sent word to his wife who was in town to prepare a nice reception for the merchants he had so generously entertained. In a hurry, the lady invited a large number of friends and arranged a wonderful banquet.

The party was a happy one, and Saladin enjoyed the unexpected hospitality. He even suspected that his identity had been discovered. Torello's wife, a tall and beautiful lady, gave them lovely gifts before they left. In short, they were literally amazed at the attention received from Torello, and Saladin departed firmly resolved to honor his host if he survived the crusade.

A few months later, the crusade was initiated, and Torello took part in it in spite of his wife's tears and entreaties. Before departing, he entrusted the wife with all the affairs of his estate and honor. While the sad lady was weeping, he asked her to promise to wait for one year, one month, and one day before marrying in case she received news of his death. She swore that she would live and die as his wife. "I know that you will," he answered. "But you are young and beautiful, and your family will pressure you to marry if you are left a widow." The lady renewed her promise, embraced him tenderly, took a ring off her finger, and gave it to him.

Torello went to the crusade and shared the fate of the rest of the Christians. Many were killed, others captured. He, too, was made a prisoner and tried to keep himself unknown. He spent his time training hawks, a skill which he mastered thoroughly. Saladin heard of his talent and took him out of prison, appointing him to the position of falconer. Neither Saladin nor Torello recognized each other.

One day Torello saw some ambassadors and sent letters to his uncle who was a respected abbot in a religious order. Meanwhile, Saladin observed a twitch in Torello's mouth that had impressed him during the incognito trip and asked him where he was from.

"I am a poor man from Pavia," Torello answered. Saladin took him into his royal residence and showed him the gifts he had received from Torello's wife among his belongings. Then he asked him if he recognized anything in the chamber.

"Nothing, except those two items that my wife gave once to some foreign merchants."

"You are Torello d'Istria!" exclaimed Saladin, embracing him tenderly. And he honored him together with all his dignitaries.

Raised to such glory, Torello paid little attention to his business in Italy. He took it for granted that his letters had been delivered to his uncle and his family was aware of his imprisonment. Actually, his wife had received different news. A certain Torello of Dignes had died during the crusade and had been buried in the camp. People confused his name with the noted gentleman Torello d'Istria and reported the sad news to his wife. She wept over his death with great sorrow. After a certain time, the chief men of her country began to seek her in marriage, and her brothers forced her to choose one of them.

By that time, Torello saw the Genoese ambassador again and asked him about his previous voyage and the letters he had delivered. A sad surprise was in store for him. The voyage had been a tragic one. The boat was destroyed, and the men perished. Torello was chagrined, for he realized that his family was not aware of his present situation and in a few days his wife's promise would expire. The poor man lost his appetite and wanted to die. Saladin heard the cause of his depression and told him to rejoice. He would deliver him back to Pavia by means of a magician capable of transferring him overnight to his town.

The following night, Saladin ordered a lavish bed set in a rich hall of his royal palace. He ordered many jewels and rich garments placed on the bed. Then he and his court took leave of Torello. The physician gave him a potion to drink and Torello fell asleep. Then the magician dispatched him instantly to the abbot's church, where he had requested to be delivered.

The next morning, the sacristan happened to see the rich bed in the middle of the church and ran away frightened. The abbot and the monks, informed of the new arrival, went into the church and were amazed at the extraordinary sight. Meanwhile, the effect of the potion wore off. Torello woke up and called to his uncle the abbot, who was fleeing with the rest of the monks.

Reassured, the abbot told Torello that everybody believed him to be dead. As a matter of fact, his wife had been forced to take a husband and the wedding was going to take place that very day. Torello and his uncle arranged that both of them would attend the nuptial celebration and see how his wife would behave. Since he was dressed in outlandish attire, Torello was introduced as a Saracen ambassador. The lady was most uncomfortable at the wedding. She did not recognize her husband in such clothes. Besides, she knew that he was dead and buried.

Torello, at the proper moment, sent a page to the lady with a special message. It was a custom in his country that at such a celebration he would drink from a cup of wine and the bride would drink the rest. The lady agreed to comply with the wishes of the stranger, who seemed to be a high dignitary. Torello put into the cup the ring he had received from his wife on his departure and drank most of the wine. When she drank the rest, she found the ring and examined it carefully. A sudden joy flooded her heart. She recognized the ring and, through it, her husband. Immediately, she took off the jewels received from the new groom, put on the ring sent by Torello, and went to embrace him eager to remain his loyal wife.

## 100.  The Patient Wife

Walter, the marquess of Saluzzo, was young, rich, and power-ful. He had neither wife nor children and spent his time hunting and hawking without any obvious intention of marrying. This kept his vassals and subjects worried about an heir to rule Walter's estates. They started to press him to find a lady of noble ancestry that might suit him. Walter told them that it was a hard thing to find a good wife, but he promised to marry as soon as he found the right woman, pro-vided that they would honor whomever he chose. This was an easy proposition for his vassals to accept.

In a village nearby there was a beautiful but poor girl whose sweet manners he appreciated. He called on her father and arranged the nuptials. Then he gathered all his vassals and announced that he was ready to honor his promise to take a wife. Again he recalled their word to accept and respect her as their lady and mistress. The day for the wedding was fixed, and the vassals all made a procession to receive the future bride with due honors.

Walter approached the poor man's house and saw his daughter Griselda coming to see who the marquess's bride would be. He asked for her father, and she told him where he was. Walter went in and told the old man he had come to marry Griselda. Then he called her and asked if she would do his will and always be obedient should he marry her. She answered yes. The marquess called the servants who carried the future bride's rich garments and ordered that Grisel-da be completely dressed with the new rich attire. After this he turned to her, as she stood shy and confused, and asked, "Griselda, will you have me as your husband?"

"Yes, my lord," she answered. He helped her mount a beauti-fully groomed horse and led her to the palace where the wedding was held with splash and merriment.

With the change of clothes, there was a total change in Griselda.

If she was beautiful before, now she looked splendid. If she was sweet, her manners now were engaging. In a short time, she gained the affection of the whole court, and those who had known her before were completely entranced. Moreover, she was so obedient and devoted to her husband that everybody agreed that he had been a wise man to marry a woman that at the very start all would respect. Her virtue was a constant topic for discussion.

In due time, she delivered a daughter which brought new happiness to Walter. But a few months later he decided to put his wife to a hard test. He goaded her with words and said that his vassals were displeased now that she had given birth to a daughter.

"My lord, I was unworthy of the dignity you have bestowed on me. Do what you please," was her calm answer. Walter felt happy with it. Yet, he still mentioned his vassals' uneasy mood and sent a man to take away the little daughter from her and pretend he would throw the baby away. She felt a sore anguish in her heart, kissed the child, and gave her away with some motherly recommendations. Walter was amazed at her patience and secretly sent the daughter to be raised by some relatives of his in Bologna.

In the course of time, Griselda begot a male child. Walter was happy at his birth, but after some time, he again complained that his vassals resented the fact that the son of a common woman might become their lord and ordered the child to be removed from her as if he would be sacrificed. Griselda felt a deep and cold pain, but behaved with the same patience as before. The little son was brought up in a magnificent way with his older sister in Bologna.

A few years later, the little girl had become a young lady, and Walter decided to give his wife a final trial. He procured counterfeit letters of dispensation from the pope and told Griselda that his marriage to her had been a mistake of his youth. He was a marquess from a powerful family and the match with a poor farm girl did not work.

"Griselda, you are no longer my wife. Take your dowry and go back to your father's home. I am taking another wife."

"My lord, I am not worthy of you and always considered whatever I received from you as a loan. Here is your nuptial ring. As to my dowry, I came naked to you. And naked shall I depart if you want the body that bore your children publicly exposed. For my lost virginity, I only ask for one sheet of my dowry."

"Granted," said Walter, who felt like crying because of his cruel experiment. Everyone around was weeping, but Walter persisted in his design.

Griselda went back home rejected after many years of faithful marriage and found still intact her old clothes. Meanwhile Walter prepared a lavish wedding pretending that he was going to marry a daughter of Count Panago. Actually, he brought back his own daughter who was a most beautiful young lady. Then he inflicted a last torture to Griselda's heart. He called her to the palace and ordered her to prepare the rooms for the new wife because he did not trust the other maids. She had to perform the job in her humble attire.

When the expected bride arrived, everybody declared that Walter had made a good exchange. Turning to his previous wife, he asked what she thought of his new bride.

"If she is as discreet as she is beautiful, she will make you very happy. But don't inflict on her the same pangs as you did on me. She would break, for she is young and delicately reared."

"Griselda, you have passed my inhuman test. You are the most patient wife and deserve to be restored to your original dignity. This girl is not my bride. She is our daughter whom you thought had been put to death. This boy is our boy. And I am your loving husband who loves you more than ever because I have the best woman in the world," said Walter, embracing and kissing his wife with tender affection.

The two children were confused and surprised at discovering their mother. The ladies, weeping, took her to a bedroom and removed her rags. Griselda was as happy as everyone else and came back to the gala with dignity. The celebration lasted a few days, which reduced the memories of the past rigor and the sharp contrast between Walter's rude wisdom and Griselda's humble greatness.

# Conclusion

Noble damsels for whom I have written this work, let me express my point of view on some objections that I have received. First of all, I have been accused of using excessive license in composing my stories and have had ladies say or hear things unbecoming to modest women. Let me tell you that this was required by the nature of the stories. Some prudes weigh words more than deeds and study to appear good rather than to be good. They resent the use of certain words. Actually, they should remember that these stories can be useful or dangerous according to the listener's disposition.

Wine is an excellent drink. Yet it harms people with high temperature. Shall we prohibit it because sick people may be hurt? Shall we ban the use of fire because it may burn homes and towns? Shall we disallow weapons, so necessary to defend peace, just because malicious men use them wrongfully? The same occurs with words. Polluted minds are contaminated, and do contaminate, through words. Look at the Holy Bible and see what happens when its venerable words are twisted. All good things, if used with wrong intentions, can be harmful. My tales will not corrupt anyone. If one is bound to do good, they will not draw him away from his purpose. Nor will they induce him to do evil if he is not inclined to do so.

There are ladies who will say that some stories should not appear in this work. Granted. But I had to reproduce all of them as they were actually told in the gathering of the ten young folks. If people pretend that I invented them—which I didn't—let me add that there is no craftsman, except God, who ever does anything equally well and equally thoroughly. Variety is unavoidable. And if some people don't like some stories, well, they can skip them and read what they enjoy.

There will be those who say that these tales are too long. The truth is that they would not read them even if they were short. I wrote them for women who have plenty of time to spend, and nothing is too long for such readers. Short writings are better suited to students who have to learn with toil rather than to ladies who read for enjoyment.

Others may say that these stories are full of quips and cranks that are unworthy of being written by a man of weight and prestige. Let me thank them, because they are moved by good intentions and concern for my reputation. I am a man of weight all right, but I am not a heavyweight. Actually, I am so light that I can float like a nutgall on water. Consider the sermons of priests and friars who rebuke men's sins. They, too, use quips in their preaching.

Again, there will be those who say that I have a poisonous tongue because I have written the truth about friars. They shall be excused because it is true that there are quite a few good friars. Concerning my tongue, I cannot trust my judgment. According to a good lady neighbor, I have the sweetest tongue of all. In any case, let me stress to those who censure me that enough has been said. Now it is time to thank Him who has led me to this end and recommend you all to His favor.

# 𝔖cripta humanistica

Directed by
BRUNO M. DAMIANI
The Catholic University of America
COMPREHENSIVE LIST OF PUBLICATIONS*

|    | *Ramiro».* | $27.50 |
| 18. | *Estudios literarios en honor de Gustavo Correa.* Eds. Charles Faulhaber, Richard Kinkade, T.A. Perry. Preface by Manuel Durán. | $25.00 |
| 19. | George Yost, *Pieracci and Shelly: An Italian Ur-Cenci.* | $27.50 |
| 20. | Zelda Irene Brooks, *The Poetry of Gabriel Celaya.* | $26.00 |
| 21. | *La relación o naufragios de Alvar Núñez Cabeza de Vaca,* eds. Martin A. Favata y José B. Fernández. | $27.50 |
| 22. | Pamela S. Brakhage, *The Theology of «La Lozana andaluza.»* | $27.50 |
| 23. | Jorge Checa, *Gracián y la imaginación arquitectónica.* | $28.00 |
| 24. | Gloria Gálvez Lira, *Maria Luisa Bombal: Realidad y Fantasía.* | $28.50 |
| 25. | Susana Hernández Araico, *Ironía y tragedia en Calderón.* | $25.00 |
| 26. | Philip J. Spartano, *Giacomo Zanella: Poet, Essayist, and Critic of the «Risorgimento.»* Preface by Roberto Severino. | $24.00 |
| 27. | E. Kate Stewart, *Arthur Sherburne Hardy: Man of American Letters.* Preface by Louis Budd. | $28.50 |
| 28. | Giovanni Boccaccio, *The Decameron.* English Adaptation by Carmelo Gariano. | $30.00 |
| 29. | Giacomo A. Striuli, *«Alienation in Giuseppe Berto».* | $26.50 |

## Forthcoming

| | | |
| --- | --- | --- |
| * | Carlo Di Maio, *Antifeminism in Selected Works of Enrique Jardiel Poncela.* | $20.50 |
| * | Juan de Mena, *Coplas de los siete pecados mortales: Second and Third Continuations.* Ed. Gladys Rivera. | $25.50 |
| * | Barbara Mujica, *Iberian Pastoral Characters.* Preface by Frederick A. de Armas. | $33.00 |
| * | Francisco Delicado, *Portrait of Lozana: The Exuberant Andalusian Woman.* Translation, introduction and notes by Bruno M. Damiani. | $33.00 |
| * | Salvatore Calomino, *From Verse to Prose: The Barlaam and Josaphat Legend in Fifteenth-Century Germany.* | $28.00 |
| * | Darlene Lorenz-González, *A Phonemic Description of the Andalusian Dialect Spoken in Almogía, Málaga — Spain.* | $25.00 |
| * | Maricel Presilla, *The Politics of Death in the «Cantigas de Santa María.»* Preface by John E. Keller. Introduction by Norman F. Cantor. | $27.50 |
| * | *Studies in Honor of Elias Rivers,* eds. Bruno M. Damiani and Ruth El Saffar. | $25.00 |
| * | Susan Niehoff McCrary, *«'El último godo' and the Dynamics of the Urdrama,»* Preface by John E. Keller. | $27.50 |

## BOOK ORDERS

* Clothbound. *All book orders,* except library orders, must be prepaid and addressed to **Scripta Humanistica**, 1383 Kersey Lane, Potomac, Maryland 20854. *Manuscripts* to be considered for publication should be sent to the same address.

www.ingramcontent.com/pod-product-compliance
Lightning Source LLC
Chambersburg PA
CBHW020353100426
42812CB00001B/44